A Comprehensive Travel Guide
to the Only Inevitable Destination

About the Author

David Staume is an observer of natural processes. The information in this book has come from his personal observations of nature and his studies in the fields of philosophy, science, metaphysics, and theosophy. He is a naturopath and herbalist, and lives in Australia with his family.

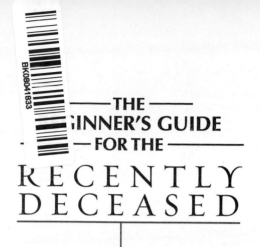

THE
ïINNER'S GUIDE
— FOR THE —
RECENTLY
DECEASED

A Comprehensive
Travel Guide
to the Only
Inevitable
Destination

David Staume

2004
Llewellyn Publications
St. Paul, Minnesota 55164-0383, U.S.A.

FIRST EDITION
First Printing, 2004

Book design and editing by Rebecca Zins
Cover image ©Digital Vision
Cover design by Gavin Dayton Duffy
Interior images from *Art Explosion 40,000* ©1995
 Nova Development Corporation

Library of Congress Cataloging-in-Publication Data
Staume, David, 1961-
 The beginner's guide for the recently deceased: a comprehensive travel guide to the only inevitable destination / David Staume.—1st ed.
  p. cm.
 ISBN 0-7387-0426-1
  1. Future life. I. Title.

BF1311.F8S78 2004
133.9'01'3—dc22

2003065810

Llewellyn Worldwide does not participate in, endorse, or have any authority or responsibility concerning private business transactions between our authors and the public.

All mail addressed to the author is forwarded but the publisher cannot, unless specifically instructed by the author, give out an address or phone number.

Any Internet references contained in this work are current at publication time, but the publisher cannot guarantee that a specific location will continue to be maintained. Please refer to the publisher's website for links to authors' websites and other sources.

Llewellyn Publications
A Division of Llewellyn Worldwide, Ltd.
P.O. Box 64383, Dept. 0-7387-0426-1
St. Paul, MN 55164-0383, U.S.A.
www.llewellyn.com

Printed in the United States of America

Contents

Preface

The Beginner's Guide for the Recently Deceased is written for the dead. If, however, you are yet to make the transition, we suggest you pour yourself a glass of wine, settle back into a comfortable chair, and let the author take you on a guided tour of the extraordinary.

Introduction

Welcome to the afterlife. My name's David, I'm your tour guide, and it's my great pleasure to be able to show you around. During this tour you are going to see some amazing things—but first, let me set the scene.

You're living in a world that's even more magnificent than the one you've come from; it's more diverse, more vivid, and more extraordinary. Your opportunities for study, exploration, and creativity are greater here than anything the physical world could offer, and your senses are enormously enhanced. There are additional dimensions of space and time, whole new kingdoms of nature, and concepts of the most extraordinary beauty and symmetry.

But the best thing about being dead is your freedom. You're free of the ground, free of the burdens of distance, free of the need to wear scuba gear to explore the oceans, and free of physical pain—to name just a few.

As glorious as this world is, though, it's not all roses and cherubs. Unpleasant things exist because they exist in our feelings and thoughts, and here these things have a vivid and objective life of their own. Post-death experiences consequently range from the sublime to the horrendous. We'll explore both ends of this spectrum, as well as the mechanism that brings them about.

We'll also discover that while death does nasty things to the flesh, it has no effect whatsoever on our prejudices. So it's possible to lead as misguided a life here as it was before you died. If you thought that physical life was all there was, you could think the same thing here. If you thought the purpose of life was to be as comfortable as possible, you could suffer that delusion as well. So while we explore where you are, what's going on, how to get around, and who and what you may bump into on your travels, we'll also explore the big questions—the whys and wherefores of existence.

As we go, I'll describe the things we see and try my best to make sense of them. So grab a harp, hop on a cloud, hold onto your sense of humor—and we'll begin.

Where the hell am I?

Most people's first and quite natural question is "Where the hell am I?" So let's begin with the fact that there is no Hell— that's Hell with a capital H. There are hells with small Hs, a variety of hellish conditions you could find yourself in—but that's no different from the physical world. The important thing is that if you find yourself in any kind of dire circumstance, it's self-created, temporary, and there's absolutely nothing to fear.

So, where the hell are you?

You probably noticed, soon after the death of your body, that you hadn't gone anywhere in space—you were pretty much in the room you died in, or around about the bus that hit you. Whether your death was peaceful, traumatic, or happened without you realizing it, all that actually occurred was that your consciousness changed focus. You were no longer focused in your physical body—you were focused in the body you have now. It's called your astral body, and the world it allows you to perceive is called the astral world.

To understand where you are, you have to recognize an important truth about your new circumstances, which is—they're not new. You may have already figured it out, but you're neither in unfamiliar surroundings nor in an unfamiliar body. There's a sense of familiarity and naturalness after death that makes it feel more like coming home, sitting down and reading your mail than any kind of journey into the great unknown. If you were expecting a long slippery tunnel to an underground hell-kitchen, death would have been a very pleasant anticlimax. But don't get complacent with all this "familiar and natural" stuff, because things are going to get pretty weird . . . and while things may be familiar, absolutely nothing is unchanged.

So, how have you changed focus to somewhere that's familiar?

Imagine that at birth you found yourself inside a car, and that it was your sole connection to the outside world—what you saw, you saw through its windows; what you felt, you felt through its suspension; and as you learned how to drive it, you found that the experiences it offered were exhilarating. Soon it became an extension of you, and you could throw it around like a rally driver. But as you thrilled to its sensations, your consciousness began to merge with it, and the line between "you" and this "extension of you" began to blur. With time you became so fused with it that you lost your sense of independent existence—your sense of identity became "I am this car," even though the proposition's as ridiculous as "I am a Volvo."

Your old physical body was such a vehicle. It was an extension of you, but it never was "you."

Before it died, you spent all day every day focused through it, but the same wasn't true of your nights— and herein lies the sense of familiarity. When vehicles sleep, their central locking releases (so to speak), and every time your physical vehicle slept, you—its driver— were free to step out. It was never a surprise where you found yourself—you were simply where you parked. Similarly, the body you found yourself in was also familiar. It was the body you always had, the body that "drove" the car.

The change of focus facilitated by your recent death was simply this, except for the fact that you're not going to wake up in it in the morning. You changed from identifying with the car, something you never were, to identifying with the body of the driver—which you're not either, but we'll explore that later.

There's an amazing fact that for some strange reason isn't widely recognized in the physical world, and that is: the major spiritual teachings, even though they arose at different times and in different cultures, actually agree on three things. Yes, I know it's a shock, but they all agree that there's a greater reality beyond physical reality; they all agree that it's possible to experience that greater reality; and they all agree that therein lies the essence of the meaning and purpose of life. Points one and two are affirmed by your presence in the astral world. There *is* a greater reality, and you're in it! The third is also true—that therein lies the essence of the meaning and purpose of life—and we will explore this throughout the tour.

Spiritual knowledge is, unsurprisingly, a little higher on the agenda in the astral world. Death is, after all, a transition that brings to mind the meaning of life, but death is most revealing by what it *doesn't* do. You don't change species, sprout wings, or suddenly become a wise spiritual being. As we've said, death has no effect whatsoever on prejudices, and so ardent bigots remain ardent bigots, and religious intolerance can poison the atmosphere here just as easily as it did in the physical world.

The essential purpose of all spiritual teachings is to ask and answer the question "Who are you?" because if you don't know who you are, you're going to miss the point of your existence entirely, and that can't be good. Over the entrance to the Temple of Apollo at Delphi were the words "know thyself," and it's the best advice you'll ever get. But to know thyself in this context isn't to know your strengths and weaknesses, your likes, dislikes, and limitations. It's to know your different bodies, your different vehicles of consciousness, the principles that govern them, and the states of consciousness revealed when you "wear" them. Understanding that you never were your old body—as obvious as that is now—is a good way to start.

Let's take a look at some of the main differences between where you are and where you've come from.

The most obvious difference between the astral and the physical world is the light. It's because the light is so special here that this world was given the name *astral*, which means "starry."

Everywhere you look there's an iridescence that surrounds and permeates everything. So much so that if I told you everything here was made of mother-of-pearl, you might even believe me. Astral matter not only bathes in this light but it also generates it. Astral matter is "self-luminous." It's also transparent to the light from the sun, so we live in a world with no shadows, not even the vast one caused by the rotation of Earth. One of the reasons that time feels different here is the absence of day and night as we knew them—a pattern that regulated our physical lives.

You may have noticed that your vision is free of the distortion of perspective—objects no longer reduce in size as their distance from you increases. Nor do objects at different distances appear to move differently from the point of view of a moving observer—a phenomena known as parallax. Some of you may have also realized that you're now able to see objects from all sides simultaneously. It's confusing at first, sometimes to the point where familiar objects are unrecognizable, but it doesn't take long to get used to it. The combined effect of these things is that your vision is extraordinarily enhanced.

There are also entirely new colors—colors that can't be described with reference to any physical ones. The astral world is a world of color—those of you who like to paint will find a far greater palette to create with. All colors appear more delicate, more radiant and alive—and they communicate more. Here, colors reveal qualities, and all qualities find expression in color. Your character is openly expressed in the colors of your astral body. The motives behind your each and every thought are as obvious as hand gestures and as readable as color-coded flags. Likewise, music can now be seen as well as heard, expressing itself in form according to its style, and color according to its emotional content.

One of the best things about being dead is getting around. It's fantastic. All you need is will, and all you have to do is enjoy the ride. Travel isn't instantaneous, but it's mighty fast. Sydney to London will only take you a few minutes with practice. It's still a matter, though, of starting at one point, finishing at another, and going through every point in between—there are no wormholes that enable you to pop up on the other side of the world instantly, but neither are there any airport customs or cramped economy-class seats. The instructions for getting around are simple—you zoom (although you can zoom at whatever pace you choose). It's like zooming in on something with a long camera lens, except that you actually go there. It happens quite naturally—just zoom, simple as that. You can't get stuck behind someone zooming slowly, nor can you explode in a shower of sparks zooming into something or someone at warp speed. There are no collisions in the astral world, it's simply not possible—and don't believe anyone who tells you otherwise. Everything passes through everything else, and does so constantly.

The only impediments to normal zooming are the planetary boundaries and our self-imposed limitations—or "silisms," as we call them. The planetary boundaries restrict us to Earth, and our silisms restrict us to the boundaries of our thought. You'll often see people walking, sometimes long distances, on the ground, purely from habit. Similarly, you'll see people walking through doorways when they could just as easily walk through the walls. In the astral world, if you think something—such as a body of water, or a wall of flame—is an obstacle, it will be.

You'll be pleased to know that one of the many freedoms here is that you don't have to work for a living. Neither food, clothing, nor shelter are the necessities they once were, and money, even if you could take it with you, is simply not the currency that gets you the best things in life. Your "work" can be pursuing whatever interests you, and there are vast opportunities for studying and exploring your fascinations. There are also plenty of opportunities for service: there are many ways you can help your brothers and sisters in the human and animal kingdoms, or, possibly, in some of the more exotic kingdoms of nature we'll look at later.

One of the things that hasn't changed, unfortunately, is the value of being multilingual, because language barriers still exist. Concrete speech is no longer required, but neither is there any "thought zapping"—you have to focus a little higher than the astral world for that—so it's still necessary to formulate whatever you're thinking in words. Because language barriers still exist, people congregate in groups just as they did in the physical world—drawn together by their common interests, beliefs, and language.

If you move about the surface of the Earth you'll see other people (with and without physical bodies), walls, desks, clocks, indoor plants, road signs, mountains—whatever you would have seen before. However, you're not seeing the physical structure—that's what your eyes were for. What you see now is their astral counterpart, the underlying structure on which their physical forms are built.

Back when you had eyes, you saw the world superficially. It was as if you were seeing a glove, but with no understanding that there was a hand inside. The glove was great to look at, pretty amazing in fact—it could wave, gesture, and catch—but, unable to see the more substantial reality underneath, you naturally attributed the substance to the bit you could see. But here, this layer of illusion is peeled away; the glove is removed. Part of the familiarity of the astral world comes from the fact that whether you see the hand or whether you see the glove, the same essential things are there.

While hands and gloves look similar at a distance, on closer inspection their differences become apparent, and it's the same with physical and astral matter. Apart from the changes brought about by the nature of the light and the significance of color, astral matter is visibly in motion. Physical matter, on the other hand, was invisibly in motion. They're so different in this regard that astral matter could be likened to a go-go dancer and physical matter to a brick.

Astral matter not only go-go dances, it's also wonderfully fluid. Being fluid, it can't be permanently injured—stabbing astral matter is as useless as stabbing water. Astral matter exhibits this fluid quality even when appearing quite coherent because it's bonded to a physical counterpart. But you could liken this to the level of a bath, where the water pouring in from the tap above and the water running down the drain below are in balance. It may *appear* static, but don't let that fool you.

Now that we've explored some of the differences between the physical and astral worlds, we're in a better position to understand our relationship to those we've "left behind." While it's natural for our physically focused friends to feel they've lost us, the feeling's not mutual because they're all in plain sight. To use the glove analogy: hands can only see other hands, and gloves can only see other gloves. You can see your old friends because you can see their astral bodies. They can't see you, however, because their vision is restricted to physical bodies. You can't see their physical bodies because hands can't see gloves. Physical matter—for us in the astral world—is as transparent as glass.

This is why we're spared the sight of our corpse. The people that hover over their "dead" body on the operating table are describing near-death experiences—not the real thing. The disadvantage, though, of not seeing your corpse, is that without this visual reference some people refuse to acknowledge that they've made the transition. Ignorance may be bliss, but these people can waste enormous amounts of time waiting to wake up!

Returning to those we've "left behind" for a moment, although we can see them, communicating with them is a different matter. While they're awake and focused in their physical body, they can neither see us nor hear us—something that's immensely frustrating and upsetting if we're watching them grieve. But during sleep the gloves are off, or, to mix metaphors, they step out of the car, and then we can not only see them, we can communicate with them—as easily as we could before we died.

If you turn your attention to the "air," you'll see that like all astral matter, it too is visibly in motion. You don't need to breathe it, not like before anyway, which is just as well, because you have no lungs. We do, however, an astral equivalent of breathing, of these tiny cells of light you can see, which we call *prana*. Prana is available to us everywhere—from the stratosphere to the ocean depths—so if one of your passions is exploring the sea, you'll find your astral body a wonderful improvement. You're not in any way limited by water pressure, you can see just as well on the deepest seabed as you can on the surface, and there's nothing to exhale—so you won't be disturbing the peace.

If you think about the diversity of life in the physical world—its tropical rainforests, sprawling cities, high altitude deserts, casinos, and temples—the breadth of life forms, landscapes, and objects was immense. In the astral world you get all this and more. This world interpenetrates the physical world and extends beyond it. The scenery and life forms you can view and study or interact with extend from below the earth's surface to about midpoint to the moon—our astral planetary boundary. The surface of Earth, the thin slice that was our physical habitat, is just one layer in a very large astral club sandwich.

But of all the different and amazing things in the astral world, the most significant is that we can now read each other's feelings and thoughts. It's particularly amazing because it means that the transition of death has turned us inside out!

When you were focused in the physical world, your thoughts and feelings were your inner reality. Only you knew what you *really* thought or felt, and your thoughts and feelings could remain hidden all your life unless you externalized them somehow, in word or deed. In the same way that stepping out of your car reveals the clothes you're wearing, death exposes your thoughts and feelings.

It isn't really that surprising, at least in retrospect. If you think back to the world you came from, you could separate reality into two aspects. Where you lived, what you owned—the material things—were your outer reality. They were objective. You could see them and feel them and others could, too. What you felt in your heart and thought in your head, on the other hand, was your inner reality. Those things were subjective. The outer reality was always more in-your-face, but the inner reality was always more influential and real. Most people miss the significance of this while they're physically alive, but it's obvious here—as it was back there when the two realities were in opposition.

Many people in the physical world had an inner reality of fear even though their fear had no objective reality. This inner reality could cause great suffering, to the point where their fears could paralyze their life. An inner reality of overweight, for example, even when the person was critically underweight, could result in starvation and death. Likewise, an inner reality of worthlessness could co-exist with an abundance of physical wealth, and drive a person to suicide. Outer realities become irrelevant when they're in opposition to how we think and feel. It's the inner reality that always drives the outcome.

It is this inner reality, how we think and feel—in essence, our character—which is externalized in death. That which was always paramount, but hidden within, is now conspicuous. Here you're seen for who you really are—and that's what we mean when we say you've been turned inside out.

To be precise, though, you've only been turned *half* inside out. While your self-centered feelings and thoughts—the product of your lower mind—have been externalized, your high ideals and unselfish thoughts haven't. These are the products of your higher mind, and they remain, for now, as inner reality. You have to wait for your "next death" to complete the process of inside-outness—but we'll come to that later.

Let's take a look at your "new" body to try to put this into context. First of all, your new body is an amazing thing—as was your physical body, of course—but this one could be described as a body of light. Although that makes it sound vastly different from the one you recently left behind, it actually isn't. All matter, even physical matter, can be described as condensed light, but this one actually looks like it.

To understand your astral body you have to see it as the blueprint upon which your physical body was built. So even though your physical body isn't around any more, the blueprint is, and it has the same essential shape. The "glove" that was your physical body looked the way it looked because it was molded by the "hand" which is your astral body. So it's easy for you to identify everyone you know, both living and dead. No one's been turned into anything generic or amorphous; in fact, the main way people look different is that they look better.

A smaller volume of astral matter extends beyond this identifiable core. It's generally in an ovoid form and it's called your aura.

When astral matter has a living physical counterpart, it generally coexists with it spatially, appearing consistent yet in constant flux, as we've seen. An exception to this is sleep. Your astral body, as a discrete vehicle of consciousness, can remove itself in sleep and death, just as a hand can remove itself from a glove. And just as gloves don't disintegrate when the hand is removed—they just go limp—physical matter does the same. Your astral and physical bodies maintained a connection in sleep, in the form of a cord that the physical body could tug on to pull your astral body and refocus your consciousness into the physical world. This was a useful feature when your bladder was full or your body heard a noise it thought you should investigate. Self-preservation is a powerful instinct in physical bodies—they could tug you back quite forcefully if they felt threatened in any way.

Your astral body, being a body of light, provides you and anyone else who cares to look with a non-stop light show. There's a continual play of color and form through your aura, corresponding with your old inner reality. In fact, you can think of your aura as your old inner reality turned inside out. The feelings, passions, desires, and thoughts of your lower mind erupt over the surface of your aura according to the intensity with which you generate them. Their intent is revealed by their features, and their nature is revealed by their colors.

The colors and features are pretty much as you'd expect. Jealousy manifests as a poisonous-looking green, depression as a miserable dull grey, love as a vibrant rose color, and hatred as black. They may be contaminated with muddy brown when selfish, a lurid red when angry, or enhanced by the sun yellow of a high intellect or the sky blue of devotion. Their intent is portrayed by their features—their forms or patterns. Cravings, for example, may manifest as hooklike tendrils, and hate as a hail of spikes. The colored forms move and mix in your aura in perfect reflection of the activity of your lower mind. So you'll see everything from auras like bubbling cauldrons of filth right through to the most exceptionally beautiful suns—if you're lucky.

While your physical body had specialized organs for each sense, your astral body is quite different. Nothing stays still long enough to support anything as stable as a nose or eyes. What exists instead are particles or units of light that constantly flow through a system of vortices called chakras. Each of these particles is a window of consciousness and, as they circulate in continual motion through your chakras, they receive the corresponding powers of perception, which we'll detail later. So astral seeing and hearing is a property of your entire body, not just of a specific part. You can therefore see equally well in front of you as behind you, as well as read the newspaper and sit on it at the same time.

To understand this and other strange phenomena we need to look at the geometry of space and time, because two extra dimensions have sprouted up around you.

The stretching of where and when

The most obvious freedom in the astral world is freedom from the heaviness and sluggishness of physical matter. It's so dramatic it's as if you're a butterfly lifted out of wet cement. Other freedoms, though, result from the less restricted geometry. Geometry is the set of rules that govern where and when. There are two additional dimensions of where and when here, and they've seriously loosened the old space-time geometry you knew and loved. They're called "rotation" and "recall."

Before your death, you were focused in a world of three spatial dimensions. Usually described in terms of various lengths, such as height, width, and depth, or latitude, longitude, and altitude, they provided the conceptual framework of "where." Armed with this concept you could define the shape of an object, locate it in space, and describe its movement in relation to something else. The fourth dimension (or first temporal dimension, if you prefer), time, was a length of a different sort—duration—and it provided the conceptual framework of "when." Armed with both concepts you could describe something in space and place it on a timeline.

Here, there's another dimension of where and another dimension of when. They get their common names from the way we generally experience them.

The additional "where" dimension is called "rotation" because you no longer have to walk around or rotate something in your hands to see all of it. Rotation enables you to see something from all sides, together with all its internal components, simultaneously. And you can see all this without in any way fragmenting your perception of the object as a whole.

This fourth spatial dimension is at right angles to the other three. Its direction is "within" and it allows you to see things closer to how they really are. In the physical world we perceived an infinity of three-dimensional space, but here in the astral world we see that this was only a "surface" compared with the infinity of the dimensions within. You're now able to see the whole of something, not just the bits that were large enough, on the surface, and happened to be turned toward you at the time.

The additional "when" dimension is called "recall," because of its effect on your perception of the past. Recall enables memory as vivid as if the event were happening again. It's more than memory—it's as if you're there. With these memories you can smell the smells and experience each and every detail, and you're able to see and feel them over and over again, in slow motion, at any particular frozen moment, and at whatever speed you like.

This means that if there's something in your past you'd prefer to forget—you can't. Recall forces you to deal with your past because it won't let you dodge it, and if your actions, feelings, or thoughts have been shameful ones, your past tends to own you, at least for a while. People with horrific pasts spend long periods of time relentlessly pursued by the horrors of their misdeeds. When you're turned inside out, your inner demons are released. But if you think that means they're going to run away into the astral wilds never to be seen again, you're wrong. While their leads are of various lengths, they're always tethered to their creator. On a brighter note, though, the beautiful memories can't be dodged either, and you'll find that they're even more glorious than they seemed at the time.

Time is also more flexible. It's easier to stretch the fabric of space-time in a medium as plastic and responsive as astral matter. In the physical realm ten seconds of something horrible could feel like an hour, or an hour of pleasure could go past in a blur. It's this stretchability of time that you'll find considerably enhanced.

If you think back to your physical life and imagine yourself in your Volvo—it was as if you were driving in a permanent U-bend, with the past curving away out of sight behind you and the future always just around the corner. But here, the additional dimension of time straightens out this U-bend, enabling you to see better in both directions. One of the things you learn here is that you were never driving into an unknown future. It may have been unknown to you at the time, but it already existed. We'll talk about the mechanism that brings this about, and how fate and free will co-exist, later in the tour.

The changes you see going on in the universe are not changes in the things themselves, but rather changes in your consciousness. Imagine that you're travelling by train through the countryside, looking through the window and watching the changing landscape. That's what the physical world was like. Now, smash the window and stick your head out—that's what the astral world is like. The first thing you realize when you stick your head out is that it's not the landscape that's changing. What's changing is your perspective. The future—the landscape ahead of you—already exists.

The perspective you saw with your physical eyes was a function of the limits of your consciousness. Where you saw birth, childhood, and adulthood flowing consecutively, in reality they exist simultaneously—in the same way as the landscape. It was your consciousness, only able to see one section at a time, which narrowed the scenery into a window frame, and gave you a timeline of past, present, and future.

We're now going to return to the subject of your astral body, because shortly after it's released from its physical counterpart, it undergoes a process of reorganization, and the effects of this can be startling.

The reorganization

Earlier, we compared the relative visible motion of astral matter to physical matter with that of a go-go dancer and a brick. Just how well astral matter go-gos, however, depends on whether it has to dance with a physical counterpart. Astral matter that doesn't have a physical counterpart can shake all it wants, but astral matter with a physical counterpart is relatively constrained. Now that your physical body has gone, and the cord we spoke about earlier has been broken, your astral body is entirely free to boogie for all it's worth. It's the ensuing shakedown that we call the *reorganization*.

Matter can be divided into categories based on relative density. In the physical world these categories were called solids, liquids, and gases. Astral matter can be similarly divided according to its relative densities, and just as physical matter has an enormous number of subdivisions within each division—different types of solids, for example—there's a similarly large number of divisions of astral matter. Your astral body can be composed of any combination of the grades of matter from this broad range.

While physical matter was moved, shaped, altered, and otherwise responsive to physical forces, astral matter is moved, shaped, altered, and otherwise responsive to feelings. Feelings, emotions, desires, and passions are powerful astral forces, and different types of feelings move different grades of astral matter. The permutations of hate, such as fear, hostility, and contempt, move the coarser grades. The permutations of love, such as reverence, respect, and compassion, move the finer grades. The grades of matter that make up your astral body are the grades of matter you've attracted to it with your feelings.

What happens in the reorganization is the same as what happens when a glass of pond water is left to stand—the particles begin to settle, migrate, and separate according to their relative densities. Released from its physical counterpart, the matter of your astral body does the same.

The heavier matter moves to the bottom of the glass, or the outer perimeter of your body, and the finer matter moves to the top of the glass, or the center of your astral body, resulting in successive layers like the rings of an onion. This doesn't occur in your aura, the ovoid where your lower mind projects itself, but in the nucleus or "identifiable you." But it doesn't change your appearance so much as filter your environment and affect the quality of your astral experience.

If, for example, you spent much of your life consumed by bitterness, you would have attracted and built into your astral body the type of astral matter responsive to this feeling. During the reorganization this matter will migrate and settle—where the coarser grades settle—in the outer layers of your astral body. The outermost layer acts as a powerful perceptual filter; like colored glass, it only allows a narrow range of experience or light through, and reflects everything else. It therefore only allows in experiences that conform to and therefore provoke this feeling—in this instance, bitterness. Your astral experiences are limited to the range of feelings to which the matter of your outermost layer can respond. This filtering is so effective that it's actually impossible to experience anything else.

The bad news is that your astral experiences begin as reflections of the worst of your character, so they begin as bad as they can get. The good news is that whatever these experiences are, they're self-created and temporary. Even the most entrenched behaviors eventually fatigue, and with time the outermost layers of your astral body dissipate, or wear away. As this happens, the matter of the layers beneath are slowly brought into play. And so your astral life, no matter how dire it is to begin, can only improve.

To see how this translates into personal experience, we'll look at two examples. In the first, we'll see a man whose physical life was dominated by the permutations of hatred—and who, in his better moments, exhibited irritability and pettiness. Then, we'll look at the astral experiences of a woman whose physical life was dominated by the permutations of love.

Due to the effects of the reorganization, we will see two entirely different astral experiences.

The man who lived his life stained by the permutations of hatred has, by his own actions, made his astral body of the coarsest materials. The effects of the reorganization on his astral life are dramatic. He is completely shut out from all but the most terrible experiences—unable to see or interact with anything or anyone not possessing the same degraded character. If he meets someone of mixed character, their better side is filtered out of his experience, and he is only able to see the worst in them. This is simply the permutations of hate he fostered internally, projected into objective reality. But this is a very real hell.

It's a self-created and finite hell, but a hell nonetheless. His mother, whom he is desperate to see, is nowhere to be found—having none of his evil characteristics, she is filtered out of his existence completely. Those he loved and who aren't filtered out only enter his world because they share some of his worst traits, and it's only these traits he can perceive. The only possibility, therefore, in any interaction, is for each party to reinforce each other's worst conceptions. At this stage of the man's astral life, every interaction is a nightmare and perpetuates his alienation.

While his mother was nowhere to be found, his enemies are always close at hand. Hate is a powerful force that binds you to those you hate. At best, this manifests as ceaseless anxiety, for his enemies have a habit of turning up wherever he goes. At worst, it manifests as pursuit. His enemies, likewise, display only their worst characteristics, reinforcing his prejudices and exacerbating his fears. If you want to be free of someone, you must neither love them nor hate them. The laws of nature are such that both love and hate create powerful bonds. To be free of someone you have to be indifferent to them.

It gets worse. He is surrounded and pressed upon incessantly by the masses of entities he has created. These are the result of a lifetime of powerful astral forces—his feelings, thoughts, and desires molding and animating the matter around him into a caravan of hideous offspring.

Once created, these entities are beyond his control. Instinctively driven by the thoughts that created them, and with a special affinity for their creator, he is quarry to their mechanical and execrable pursuit. As if being hunted by your own creations isn't enough, the dimension of recall allows him no respite from the vivid replay of his crimes.

For this man, there is no such thing as a single moment of peace. The reorganization has formed a harsh perceptual filter around him, and he will live in this state for as long as the filter remains—a period corresponding to the intensity with which he created it. Hell is simply a hole one digs for oneself.

But if you think this is like being tied to a chair and made to watch a bad movie, you're very much mistaken. Emotions and desires are experienced here with hugely increased intensity, and all this is very real. A substantial loss of power occurs in the translation of feelings, emotions, and desires into physical existence, but here, in their element, their power is undiminished. There is no physical pain in the astral world—the agony of hell is emotional pain, but it can be as debilitating as a sledgehammer to the heart.

Fortunately, though, there's no such thing as eternal damnation—just the finite consequences of finite actions. As the coarsest matter of his astral body dissipates—through conscious effort or mere hate-fatigue—his world becomes brighter, by degrees. Eventually, the matter corresponding to the lower selfish emotions—gossip, irritability, pettiness, and arrogance—come into play, and the man's astral life gradually replaces horror with emotional dross.

This process of slow improvement continues until his astral experience corresponds to his highest emotional achievement—the love he may have expressed to a family member, for example. And so his experience will range from horror to glimpses of exceptional beauty. In all of it, though, he simply reaps what he has sown.

That's about as bad as it's ever likely to get. At the other end of the spectrum, fortunately, astral life is joyous and overflowing with opportunities.

The woman whose life was dominated by the permutations of love has a wholly different astral experience. When her inner reality externalizes, a beautiful and peaceful world unfolds. The reorganization still occurs, such as it can, but any filtering would be minimal and short-lived. And so all the vast possibilities, freedoms, and beauty of this world are hers. Having none of the coarsest grades of matter in her body, she can have no experience of hell. None. She can study it if she wants, as an observer, but not as a participant. In fact, she's completely protected from all the permutations of hatred.

To understand why this is so, we need to take a look at thoughtforms.

As we've seen, feelings, desires, and emotions are powerful astral forces. They seize, mold, and energize astral matter to produce actual entities. With their blind instinct and temporary lives, these entities behave a lot like viruses. Like viruses, their purpose in life is to reproduce themselves. To do so they need to dock with a host, and for that there has to be an affinity that enables a way in. For a thoughtform to dock and discharge itself there has to be astral matter in its target that's capable of response. Thoughtforms whose instincts are to reproduce lower feelings, such as irritability, for instance, require coarser grades of matter. Thoughtforms whose instincts are to reproduce higher feelings, such as tolerance, require finer grades of matter. If this correspondence or affinity exists, the thoughtform will dock, discharge its contents, and reproduce itself. What is reproduced by thoughtforms, though, is the feeling, the feeling that gave birth to it in the first place.

Say, for example, you desire alcohol. Your desire will create thoughtforms whose purpose in life is to reproduce the feeling "I desire alcohol." If this feeling is self-centered, as this is, your astral offspring will never go far away. As its creator, you have the requisite affinity, the right stuff in your aura, because you made it in the first place. So it can dock at any time, and it will take this opportunity whenever you're not focused on something else. With your selfish thoughtforms hanging around and encroaching upon your every unfocused moment, it's very easy for habits to form—for each thought along a particular path makes the next step along that path more likely.

There's another reason for this particular example, because you can't drink—not like you used to, anyway. You've lost the internal plumbing. What you haven't lost, though, is the *desire* to drink. Add this to the fact that feelings are intensified in the astral world and you can begin to appreciate the dilemma. Much of the suffering in the astral world comes from the unleashing of powerful desires that simply cannot be satisfied.

There are so many thoughtforms in the astral world that it's like swimming in an ocean full of jellyfish, and if you have the right stuff in your aura you'll feel them brush against you constantly. But this is different from "feeling" in the physical sense. You can't touch the surface of anything with your astral body—

everything interpenetrates everything else—so there's no hard or soft, nor rough or smooth. On coming into contact with something, what you feel is its vibration, which you then interpret—as pleasant or unpleasant, stimulating or depressing, for example.

Imagine zooming through masses of thoughtforms all docking and discharging. It's enough to drive you crazy—unless, of course, you're immune. Immunity is conferred by weeding out the corresponding grades of matter from your astral body. For example, if you weed out the permutations of hatred from your character, you'll be immune to those thoughtforms. Now we can see why the woman of virtue is effectively protected from all evil. With no affinity in her astral body, there's no way in—no docking point. She's immune. As far as evil influence is concerned, she doesn't exist.

Perhaps we should put the word "evil" into context here, because the astral world gives us a broader perspective. It seems that nothing is, of itself, either good or evil. What bends something one way or the other is the use and motives behind its use. In the broad and true scope of things, evil is seen as "undeveloped good," and in all of life's situations, in all the worlds, it must neither be feared nor compounded.

Let's take a look now at what happens when we send thoughtforms to someone else.

All thoughtforms act out the impulse that generated them, doing what they're created to do for however long they hold together. When directed at someone else, they zoom to their target, dock (if possible), then discharge and reproduce themselves, as normal. But if no affinity exists, the thoughtform is unable to dock, and it returns to its creator. A good thoughtform sent to the undeserving will therefore return as a blessing. A harmful thoughtform sent to the virtuous, however, returns with the equivalent of a hard slap to your own face. The woman of virtue is therefore not only protected from evil, she has the most perfect counterattack, of which she'll be entirely oblivious.

The virtuous woman has access to all the wonders the astral world has to offer. Protected from evil and free of the thoughtforms that encrust the morally weak, she is always at peace. With unfettered access to every corner of this magnificent realm, her possibilities for enjoyment and progress are greater in every way than in the physical world. She can pursue any virtuous passion; she can explore, learn, or help, and all with immunity from harm. She can explore the wonders of the earth without having to dig, the depths of the oceans without a submersible, and the textures of clouds without having to plummet through them on a sky dive. She can listen to the grandest music, with the added bonus of seeing it expressed in form and color. She is able to observe and learn about the non-human lines of evolution that inhabit this world, with excellent odds of not scaring them away. She may devote herself to her interests in science, philosophy, art, or literature, and be able to draw correlations hitherto only alluded to by poets. She'll see causes where previously she saw only effects, and she'll be able to look directly into the living book of nature, as well as into other libraries beyond her wildest dreams. She can continue her philanthropic work with more vigor and effect than ever before. She can see any of her astral friends in any country within minutes, and her physical friends whenever they're focused in their astral body. Through all these and other opportunities she'll improve her knowledge—of herself, and the worlds around her—and progress spiritually.

Let's take a look now at the spectrum of people and other life forms she could metaphorically bump into on her travels.

It's a difficult task taking a census in the astral world—no one sleeps, everyone interpenetrates everyone else, and top speeds reach thousands of miles a minute. However, every few years the Astral Bureau of Statistics manages to compile their "Who's Who and What's What in the Astral World." We'll use their classification system and take a look around.

The ABS classifies seven primary groups of life forms: Minerals, Plants, Animals, Nature Spirits, Artificial Entities, Humans, and Devas.

Mineral life is the most constrained form in which evolving life is found. As physical matter presents no obstacle to you, your ability to explore and study this kingdom is immensely improved. You can compare tectonic plates across continents, zooming from one to the other in minutes, to see how landmasses were joined in the past and have moved over time. You can admire the magnificence of this kingdom's highest achievements—the precious and semi-precious stones and metals—and you can study their manufacture. You can grimace at the enormous pressures under which minerals begin to experience sensation and you can marvel at the evolutionary pathway that cycles them in and out of the bodies of plants. You can look for buried treasure, buried civilizations, the remains of dinosaurs undisturbed under meters of silt, and all without having to dig or dirty your clothes.

Plant life can be explored under the sea with the peace and convenience of not having to breathe. You can study their structure in microscopic detail without the limitations of a microscope. You can see in their astral bodies the development of sensation, their pleasure or discomfort, and their ability to recognize changes in their environment. You can interact with the developing personalities of the longer-lived species, such as the grand old trees. You can study the evolutionary pathway that cycles them in and out of the bodies of animals and humans. You can admire the magnificence of their highest achievement—flowers—and study their relationships with animals and nature spirits. You can listen to the warning "hungry caterpillar approaching" and watch it relay like tom-toms through the jungle.

Unlike the mineral and plant kingdoms, the animal kingdom isn't rooted to the spot. If you thought they could move fast in their physical bodies, you should try catching one in its astral body! Some are instinctively drawn to humans for their own evolutionary purposes, but most instinctively avoid your average irritable human aura. Add the fact that many arrive here from a death at human hands and you'll see why many animals present problems of observation and interaction. But they're the ones without physical bodies—the ones with physical bodies can be studied from the astral perspective as they go about their physical lives, but you can't interact with them when they're focused elsewhere. A calm and beautiful aura, however, gives you a good chance of observing and interacting with astral animals, which you may do in the intimacy of their burrows or soaring beside them on the wing.

You can study the different lines of evolution that take some animals into the human kingdom and some into the realm of the nature spirits. You can fly with flocks of geese and observe them feel and act in synchronicity, moved by their communal soul. You can watch as masses of murdered animals are released into the astral world after satisfying the physical world's appetite for meat. You can observe the progress of animals fortunate enough to come into close association with benevolent humans, and study the evolutionary pathway along which communal souls progress toward the attainment of individual self-consciousness. Some animals achieve this by entering the pathway of human evolution, but there are other evolutionary pathways, particularly for the animals of the sea and the air, which take them into the kingdom of the nature spirits.

Nature spirits belong to a distinct but parallel evolution to our own and generally attain their individual self-consciousness through entering into the kingdom of the devas. Here we find the fairies, gnomes, water spirits, pixies, elves, trolls, goblins, and sylphs of mythology. There are a large number of groups and subgroups of nature spirits in the "Who's Who"—and they vary in character, appearance, and intelligence to the same extent that animals and humans do.

Finding your average human rather repulsive, nature spirits generally shrink from human contact. You can probably imagine that if a troll thinks you're ugly, you've got some serious work to do to improve yourself! However, if your aura's beautiful and serene, there are opportunities for studying these exotic creatures. To be "off with the pixies" is, in fact, an enormous privilege.

You'll find nature spirits are territorial, preferring their own particular natural habitats: mountains, gardens, shallow seas, or fields. They're given broad groupings according to their affinities with the four elements, and so you see categories of nature spirits referred to by the terms "earth, water, air, and fire"—denoting their preferred environment. Generally benevolent, graceful, brilliantly colorful, and often with the ability to change shape at will, one of their favorite occupations is watching and participating in the processes of nature. And so you'll find them attending the opening of flowers, snowboarding falling snowflakes, riding waves, and helping beetles that have fallen on their backs to right themselves.

Nature spirits are fun loving and often mischievous. Another of their favorite pastimes is animating some of the various thoughtforms that attract their attention. Most people don't see the humor when they're the target of one of these pranks—and humans invariably are their targets—but they bring a great deal of humor to the astral world.

There was a man who created an elaborate thoughtform, while he was physically alive, of St. Peter at the gates of Heaven. Shortly after he died, he encountered his creation, but—as is normally the case—he had no idea that he had created it. A nature spirit promptly animated the form of St. Peter and denied the man entry to Heaven on the grounds that he was too short. Although this was done without malice, it had a damaging effect on the man until he could be persuaded it was a joke.

Many séances and readings by low-grade clairvoyants in the physical world involve nature spirits reading the thoughts of those present and working those insights into some inane prophecy. The thought is then passed to the clairvoyant, who considers it a product of his or her intuition. It's enormous fun, and a very popular astral pastime, with crowds of nature spirits gathering around and howling with laughter.

Most of the artificial entities in the astral world are of humankind's unconscious creation. They're the thoughtforms we've discussed—our desires and thoughts molding astral matter into temporary beings. These entities live out their temporary lives doing what they were created to do. However, like bullets fired from a gun, once they've been fired they're beyond the control of their creator. En masse, thoughtforms represent popular community and national feelings, with the powerful ability to color our thinking or subvert the process completely. We were particularly vulnerable to these prejudices when we had physical bodies because we couldn't see them. If an affinity existed they'd dock, discharge, and reproduce themselves. Knowing no better, we'd think the feeling or thought that arose was our own. Because of this we'd often dwell on it, reinforce and perpetuate it, when almost all such thoughts should be instantly dismissed.

The ABS classifies the human population into those with sleeping physical bodies, those with physical bodies who have developed astral consciousness, and those without physical bodies. Overlaying these are three broad levels of human development: young humans, developing humans, and advanced humans. Beyond advanced humans are two specific groups: adepts (perfected humans) and their disciples. Trying to describe the diversity of the human population in the astral world is even more difficult than doing it in the physical world, so a sprinkle of examples will have to do.

At any given time, about a third of the human population of the physical world are here in the astral world as "sleepers." They are generally self-absorbed in the process of acting out their fears and fantasies in their self-created inside-out world. As all their fears are unnecessary, and most of their fantasies are projections from their lower chakras—something we'll explore later—their astral episodes are generally self-indulgent wastes of time. Except for the fact that physical bodies regenerate when consciousness is absent, most sleep is wasted. On waking, sleepers encounter the considerable difficulties inherent in a four-dimensional physical brain (three of space and one of time) trying to grapple with a six-dimensional memory (these, plus rotation and recall). The result is usually either a blank, or a strange and rapidly disintegrating movie.

For a person whose life was dominated by the basest of sensations, the transition of death is devastating. Even when attending their own funeral, denial is common, and the desire to return can be desperate and terrible. Here and there in the astral world you'll find what are termed "bottom dwellers"—those with powerful and unresolved physical appetites. They include drunkards, the violent, the perverse, or those simply unwilling to accept the loss of their body. The term "bottom dweller" is used for two reasons: one metaphorical and the other, unfortunately, all too literal.

Your average bottom dweller is found in the lowest astral environments, those closest to the physical, haunting all the places they would have haunted in physical life. The combination of powerful physical desires with the impossibility of satisfaction leads them to search for people with physical bodies that they can influence or possess. Their search begins by looking for people with desires similar to their own—which is easy enough when you can see auras—and if they're lucky they'll find someone with a base chakra that's weak enough to allow them in.

The gates to the base chakra are weakened by a range of factors, including alcohol and other drugs, certain mental states, the loss of the will to live, and moral weakness. On finding a sufficiently weak base chakra, bottom dwellers will try to access their host's physical senses, and so feel "alive" again—at least by their definition. If their host's will is sufficiently weak, the relationship may endure, the bottom-dweller adhering to their host like a remora—one of the more dreadful astral sights you'll see—and encouraging them to the excesses they indulged in prior to their death.

Here we find an argument to add to a long list against capital punishment. Someone who has committed a terrible crime, especially if at risk of recidivism, should not be launched into the astral world. It's relatively easy for the immoral and resourceful among us to influence the minds of young or developing humans in the physical world. Susceptible or like-minded individuals are easy to find when auras are visible and character is obvious, and being unaware of the possibility of such influence makes these people particularly vulnerable. The physical world achieves far more protection for its inhabitants through the incarceration and rehabilitation of criminals than it does by letting them loose here.

Suicides find, of course, that they haven't "ended it all" at all. The cruel world they attempted to leave has not gone away, and nor have their problems. The only thing that's gone is the opportunity to physically work through them. Fortunately, there are many wonderful people here to help them, and they rarely lack the offer of friendship and post-death counseling. The fact is, we incarnate for a purpose, and our natural instinct for self-preservation should be observed so that the lessons of physical life can be learned.

There's a very small group of humans whom we generally won't see, but should mention—those rare and wonderful humans who experience little or no astral consciousness after their physical death. The astral world is only a pit stop on life's highway. Most of us remain here only for the purposes of wearing out the consequences of our selfishness. Once that's done we experience our next death and move on. Yes, just when you thought you'd had enough, the Grim Reaper has another lunge at you. Those rare individuals who have no selfishness to weed out pass through with little or no conscious astral life, and move on to states of being that leave this place for dead.

Talking about rare individuals, the evolutionary ladder of the cosmos has beings younger than us on its lower rungs, and beings older than us on its higher rungs. At the top of our small section of the ladder are perfected humans, called adepts. Adepts are the leaders of human evolution. They are great beings who have unfolded near to the limits of human potential.

Adepts have conquered death. Their consciousness is seamless throughout the realms of nature, and their wisdom, love, and power are supreme in human terms. They can change focus from the physical world to the astral world and beyond, to superior realms of consciousness as easily as we focus from our hand to the horizon. They clearly perceive what's right and what's wrong, and always choose what's right, irrespective of the apparent consequences. They know what's important and what's not important, are steadfast in all that's important, and yielding in all that is not.

Adepts have eliminated all personal desire and act wholly as their higher selves. They are always kind, gentle, and accommodating, allowing others the liberty they expect for themselves. They are able to draw into their bodies the vast spiritual energies of the cosmos, and have consequently fully awakened their highest senses. Morally impeccable, masterful in their use of the laws of nature, beyond the necessity for rebirth, and liberated from all suffering, their lives, to us, are incomprehensible. Those that remain in close communication with human evolution are referred to as masters.

Devas, or angels, comprise a kingdom of nature further along the evolutionary pathway of the nature spirits, in the same way that humans are further along the evolutionary pathway of the land animals. Their evolution is distinct from our own, and as a kingdom of nature they are significantly more advanced. Most devas live in realms superior to the astral and rarely interact with this world, but the lower subgroups can be seen here from time to time.

Devas have bodies with a typical and unmistakable fiery quality. Their countenances radiate nobility and benevolence, and their auras can extend immense distances. No human language can describe the majesty of the highest of their forms. Perhaps only their own language of color and music can do that, but a glimpse may be possible. Imagine a solar flare leaping from the surface of the sun as a mere flash of their bloomers as they do the can-can, and you'll be selling them short. It's probable that the highest of their kind reach levels of existence way beyond the reach of even the greatest of humankind's spiritual teachers.

It's time now to turn our attention to the deepest and most fundamental things we know.

The Enfolded All

In the physical realm there's a common misconception that merely because someone's here—in the next world—they're bestowed with some form of higher understanding. Alas, no. Asking the meaning of life around a Ouija board is no better than asking the same question around a card table. Part of the sense of familiarity and naturalness of this realm comes from the fact that no miracles occur just because you stop breathing. Conversations here can be just as inane and lives can be just as meaningless, indulgent, sad, and generally dysfunctional as physical ones.

Having said that, you'll find that there is more knowledge here because there's an increased capacity to know, and although there's no compulsory higher understanding, there is more wisdom. The ability to look back on a life just lived helps, as does the soul-searching provoked by the broad range of experiences that we create for ourselves. However, despite all this, it's still true that only a small proportion of people have awakened to the meaning and potential of their existence. The interesting thing is, the answer is all around us—all we have to do is draw the connections.

With your increased capacity to see, take a look at this flower. Look at the majesty of its form. Look at the way it radiates light and the way it expresses itself in color. Look at how it creates images of itself and sends them out to communicate with bees and noses. It's a creation of the most exceptional beauty, and it beautifully illustrates the meaning and potential of existence.

But before you get too excited by the analogy, you're not the flower—you're this hard, green bud further down the stem. Hardly comparable, you may think, but the flower is enfolded in the bud. The process that realizes the flower within is called unfolding. Unfolding means opening up and turning inside out, revealing all that exists within. You're unfolding like the bud, and your recent experience of turning inside out is part of this process. The process of unfolding is also known as evolution.

Now I guess you're aware that you're not on your way to becoming a chrysanthemum. So what *are* you on your way to becoming? What's enfolded in you? What does evolution have in store? To answer this, we have to explore the fundamentals of the universe. We have to know something of the structure of reality, and that involves mathematics. But this is a beginner's guide, so we're not going to be doing differential calculus or quadratic equations, we're simply going to count very slowly on our fingers.

Before we can raise our first finger, though, there has to be a fist, a conveniently almost-round fist representing zero, nothing. Nothing unfolded, that is. You see, "nothing" means "no things," nothing yet realized in form—but everything, absolutely everything, enfolded. Behind all that exists, before any thing can exist, there's this. We'll call it the Enfolded All.

Now there's not too much we can really say about the "Enfolded All"—only slightly more than nothing, in fact—and even if we had much to say, language tends to fall apart. But we can't let a little thing like being potentially completely unintelligible stop us, so we'll express what we can.

We can say, "All existence originates from the Enfolded All"—in the same way that your fingers originate from your fist.

We can also say, "None of existence is separate from the Enfolded All"—in the same way that your fingers aren't separate from your fist.

We can also say, "Existence is a process whereby the ideals held in the Enfolded All develop and unfold." "Ideal" is used here in its meaning of "an archetypal idea or pattern."

And lastly, we can say, "Existence is a periodic event." At some point it will enfold and return to the Enfolded All as the seed of a future cosmos.

Those four statements show the limitations of our knowledge. The Enfolded All could also be called the "Unmanifest Progenitor of the Cosmos" or "Source of Existence," and you may rightly refer to the Enfolded All as "God." But this is not the god of limited imaginations. This is a being whose will reveals itself as the laws of nature, whose ideas work themselves out as evolution, and whose body is the cosmos. This is not a god who can in any sense be appeased, implored, or persuaded. This is not a god who favors any one being or any one religion over another, makes arbitrary decisions to reward or punish, or can be conscripted to any cause—so it's quite all right if you're an atheist about *that* god.

Pythagoras taught that at its deepest level, reality is mathematical. So now that we have nothing, we shall begin to count.

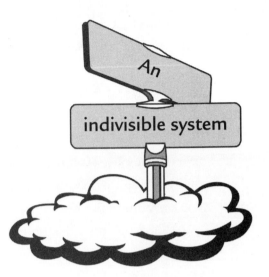

The ideals of the Enfolded All exist as a unity—and that's our cue to unfold a finger and count to one. Here our knowledge is a little stronger and language holds together a little better.

The cosmos—in its ideal state, unrestricted by geometry—is a unity, an indivisible system, a reality where all is one. As we raise our consciousness, we see that fragmentation—the state of one thing being separate from another thing—is solely a function of geometry, the dimensions that constrict our existence, and that these dimensional restrictions can be transcended. What that actually means is nothing is in any real sense separate from anything else.

Conceiving an indivisible system is mind-bendingly difficult, but we can try to approach an understanding of it in a number of ways. Imagine a system comprised of a gazillion tiny points in space. Now imagine each and every one of those points expanding, interpenetrating, "knowing" their neighbor, expanding until each and every one becomes indistinguishable from the system as a whole. None of these expanded points could then be distinguished from any other, and none could be said to have a different location from any other. So the center of the system would be everywhere, and its circumference would be nowhere. No matter how you tried to carve it up, each part would contain the whole. Even smashing it into a gazillion pieces couldn't give you a "this bit" and a "that bit."

If that crashed your hard drive, then reboot and try this. Maybe you've seen a hologram. If so, what you saw was a three-dimensional image produced by shining a laser beam through holographic film. To create this film you split a laser beam in two, aim one beam at the object to be photographed and the other off to the side. The first beam bounces off the object to be photographed and into the path of the second beam. This creates an interference pattern and it's this that's recorded on the film. To the naked eye the film looks like a pattern of raindrops falling on a puddle, but shining a laser through this film reproduces the photographed object as a hologram, a projected three-dimensional image. The interference pattern is an indivisible system. If you cut the film in half and shine a laser through one of the halves, the whole image appears. Cut it in half again, and again, and still the whole image appears. Slicing the film into a dozen pieces still won't give you a "this bit" and a "that bit," as every portion contains the information of the whole.

Our wonderful cosmos is such a system, an indivisible system. Fortunately, no matter how poor our descriptions or weak our analogies, the two principles that arise from this are clear: first, nothing is in any sense truly separate from anything else; and second, the whole is enfolded in every part.

The first principle means we are in no way separate from the world. Any perceived separation in the cosmos is an illusion. Although we perceive separate "things," they're like rain, steam, snow, rivers, and clouds—all water, all somewhere in the cycle of either issuing from or returning to the sea, and separate from it only in appearance.

Here in the astral world our consciousness is a little closer to the indivisible reality than it was in the physical world. The geometry here is less restricted, which makes this world less fragmented. As a consequence, some of the layers of illusion of the physical world are peeled away. Many things that were separate in the physical world merge in the astral world quite naturally.

Sight, hearing, taste, and smell, for example, once the domain of eyes, ears, mouths, and noses, merge with the loss of individual receptors. To your new senses, the bark and smell of a dog are inextricably interwoven with how it is seen. So to hear is to see, to smell is to hear, and to see is to smell. Another example is forwards, backwards, and sideways as they pertain to perception and movement. Someone can't sneak up behind you when you have no behind. When you can see, hear, smell, and taste simultaneously—and in all directions simultaneously—the terms lose their meaning. It's called the Trinidad and Tobago phenomenon—

drain away the Caribbean Sea and they're simply knuckles on the same fist!

It's no different from when things previously seen as separate and distinct in the physical world were revealed by physics to be facets of the same thing, such as matter and energy, electricity and magnetism, space and time, gravitation and acceleration, waves and particles. The physical world was like a jigsaw puzzle dropped on the floor. Although not separate from the indivisible reality in any way, you could describe the physical world as what an indivisible reality looks like when projected through a series of successively restrictive geometries. With each new dimensional restriction the world is shattered into separate and lesser parts—like a three-dimensional die unfolded to become six two-dimensional squares, with all their interrelationships lost in the process.

The second principle that arises from an indivisible system is "the whole is enfolded in every part." And you're included in that "every part" bit. You may feel as if you're just a drop of water, but you literally have the whole sea enfolded within you. We can now answer the question we raised a little while ago. What's enfolded within you, waiting to be realized, is not a chrysanthemum—it is nothing less than the unimaginable glory and beauty, capacity and wisdom of the cosmos. Seriously! But don't hold your breath; it could take a while to unfold.

And if you think that's amazing, couple it with its corollary. The corollary of "the whole is enfolded in every part" is that the principles of any one part are reflected in all the others. This is called the Law of Correspondences. We'll explore this in detail later on, but a result of this law is that we can know the cosmos simply by opening our eyes and drawing connections. For example, the life cycle of the cosmos is readable in the life cycle of a tree.

A tree is a periodic manifestation that begins as a seed, enfolded with all the ideals of its progenitor. Its life is a process of unfolding these ideals into realization. It may or may not accomplish these within any one lifetime, but the purpose of its existence is clear—to strive to unfold them. At various times in its life process it will enfold the ideals back into seeds so that a period of manifestation may arise again. All existence is engaged in this process—you, me, the tree, and the cosmos as a whole.

As the core of reality is a unity, those who see unity will always be closer to the truth than those who see division. The things people have in common will always outweigh their differences, and their differences are simply the product of the illusion of fragmentation. To see things as they really are, we have to see through this. The first important step is to realize it intellectually. To experience it, though, we have to consciously integrate ourselves into the world, dissolving the intellectual and emotional distinctions that separate subject from object. As we integrate ourselves into the world, realms of successively liberated geometry open up to us. As this occurs, separate things merge and our knowledge of the universe and ourselves expands.

Unification, therefore, progresses our evolution. It unfolds the cosmos within us and expands our consciousness toward the indivisible reality. The power of unification, the power to put all the jigsaw pieces together to see the whole picture, is love.

Love: permeating the cosmos, dissolving the illusion of fragmentation, progressing our evolution, expanding our consciousness; all this and warm and cuddly, too. Let's take a look at the permutations of love—and while we're at it we'll take a look at its alter ego, hate.

If you encourage feelings of love, your consciousness expands. You grow larger. You open up to the world around you. You see, love is a force of attraction, but it doesn't pull things toward you so much as expand you so that you encompass them. Love, the force of unification, is the driving force of evolution. Pulling us together, defragmenting us, love brings our consciousness closer to God.

Love has many permutations, but they can be classified according to the relationship between the subject and the object. If you perceive the object of your love as being greater than you, love will manifest as reverence. Reverence can be seen as love looking up, and may be displayed in forms such as worship, esteem, or admiration. If you perceive the object of your love as being equal to you, love will manifest as affection. Affection can be seen as love looking at its own level, and may be displayed in forms such as comradeship, friendliness, or respect, the common characteristic being the desire for mutual help. If the object of your love is perceived as being lower than you, love will manifest as benevolence. Benevolence can be seen as love looking down, and may be displayed in forms such as compassion, kindness, or pity. We're talking about love here, so the terms "greater," "equal," and "lower" are meant in an evolutionary sense—and so "lower," in this context, simply means that they're a younger soul.

If, on the other hand, you encourage feelings of hate, your consciousness contracts. You grow smaller. You close down to the world around you. Hate is a force of repulsion, but it doesn't push things away from you so much as shrink you so that you disengage from them. Hate, as a force of fragmentation, stalls our evolution. Pushing us apart, fragmenting us, it takes our consciousness further from God. But it can only do so temporarily; it can never disengage us from that which we are intrinsically part of. Not even hate can divide an indivisible reality.

While hate is a powerful force of repulsion, it can do no more than temporarily stretch the rubber band that binds subject and object together. The greater the hatred, the greater the stretch, and therefore the harder the rubber band will eventually recoil. As long as hate exists, subject and object will stretch apart, only to inevitably smack back into each other, then repulse again, stretch apart, and then recoil and knock each other out, et cetera et cetera *ad infinitum*. The only way to stop this cycle is to eliminate the force of repulsion.

Hate also has many permutations, and they can be similarly classified according to the relationship between the subject and the object. If you perceive the object of your hate as being greater than you, hate will manifest as fear. Fear can be seen as hate looking up, and may be displayed in forms such as dread, anxiety, or apprehension. If you perceive the object of your hate as being equal to you, hate will manifest as anger. Anger can be seen as hate looking at its own level, and may be displayed in forms such as hostility, insolence, or coldness, the common characteristic being the desire for mutual harm. If you perceive the object of your hate as being lower than you—which in the context of hate means "inferior"—hate will manifest as arrogance. Arrogance can be seen as hate looking down, and may be displayed in forms such as contempt, superciliousness, or tyranny.

The permutations of hate retard our evolution, because hate perpetuates the illusion of separation. Hate is therefore a sign of ignorance—ignorance of the way forward. For that reason, though, the perpetrators of hate are worthy of compassion.

The first unsurprising consequence of an indivisible reality fragmenting is duality. Love and hate are a duality, but they're not *the* duality . . . and that sounds like a good time to unfold another finger and count to two.

The emissive

and the receptive

The basic function of your astral body is the same as all your other bodies—to give and receive a select band of energies from the environment. To do this, you have to be able to give and you have to be able to receive. Welcome to the fundamental duality—the essence of giving and receiving—also known as yin and yang, or the emissive and receptive principles.

It seems that the cosmos is woven with just two threads. Yin is the receptive principle. Its essence is that of emptiness, a state that necessarily draws in and fills. Yang is the emissive principle. Its essence is that of fullness, a state that necessarily gives out and empties.

To understand your astral body, or any other body for that matter, you have to understand the mechanism by which it gives and receives from its environment. To use your astral body to the fullest, you have to know when and how to make certain parts of it receptive, and when and how to make certain parts of it emissive.

Let's imagine unity as a large rubber sheet, held at its corners so that it's vertical and taut. Whenever force is applied to it, the rubber sheet is pushed or pulled one way or another, and whenever this occurs, the unity becomes a duality—in this instance, a duality of concave and convex.

The concave side demonstrates the receptive principle. As it forms, it creates an emptiness that draws in and fills. The convex side demonstrates the emissive principle. As it forms, it creates a fullness that pushes out and empties. As with all dualities, the receptive and emissive principles are dependent on and in opposition to each other; they cannot exist without each other, and they cease to exist in equilibrium. They must live together or die together, like Romeo and Juliet.

It may seem obvious to say that we need to know how and when to receive and how and when to give, but it's rarely considered conceptually, and not often applied and practiced universally. Neither are they just concepts for us to recognize so we can watch them weave the cosmos. The mastery of their use is said to be the greatest power in creation.

If you're in the presence of purity, beauty, wisdom, or love, you need to know how to be appropriately receptive or you will fail to be enriched. When communicating with an audience, you need to know how to be appropriately emissive or you will fail to be heard. Likewise, you can repel harmful acts, feelings, and thoughts by being appropriately emissive, and you can learn to seek and receive beneficial acts, feelings, and thoughts by being appropriately receptive. You can also learn the art of equilibrium, or neutrality, of being uninvolved and disinterested in acts, feelings, and thoughts, and thus neither push nor pull the fabric of reality. With neutrality you can walk though a tempest and neither affect it nor be affected by it. Observing the receptive and emissive principles sheds light on all of life's mysteries, and as you develop and apply these principles with your will, the potential for your interactions with the cosmos defies the imagination.

Let's take a look at some examples of the emissive and receptive principles in operation.

Back when you had a physical body, your in-breath was receptive, a passive movement where air was drawn in to fill your lungs. Your out-breath was emissive, an active movement where muscles contracted and your lungs were emptied. The two states were dependent on and in opposition to each other, and one couldn't exist without the other.

The female sexual organs are receptive, designed to open, draw in, and receive. Male sexual organs are emissive, designed to penetrate, give, and empty. Masculinity and femininity are dependent on and in opposition to each other, and one cannot exist without the other.

Black holes are receptive, the equivalent of a cosmic in-breath, drawing in everything, including light. Stars are emissive, the equivalent of a cosmic out-breath, giving light and a wide range of other sustaining energies as they discharge. They're similarly dependent on and in opposition to each other, and one cannot exist without the other.

Your chakras work in the same way. We mentioned them briefly a while ago, as a system of vortices in your astral body, and we'll look at them in detail soon.

They're suns and black holes in microcosm—your training wheels for that far-off day when suns and black holes will truly be parts of your body. When we say "the whole is enfolded in every part," we really mean it. If you think it would be fun to have a solar system named after you, just imagine how much fun you could have *being* one!

The force that creates duality—that pushes or pulls the fabric of reality to create the cosmos and realize the ideals of the Enfolded All—is the same force that you use to make things happen: will. As an operation of the will, every action, emotion, desire, and thought distorts the fabric of reality. All that exists is the result of the action of will; either the will of the Enfolded All or such will as has unfolded within its cosmos. Your will is the faint glow unfolded within you of a minute portion of the will of the Enfolded All.

The image of the rubber sheet, concave on one side and convex on the other, is dynamic. Its concave side wants to push back out and its convex side wants to pull back in—to equilibrium. In the physical world this law is known as Newton's Third Law: When one object exerts a force on another, there's an equal and opposite reaction on the first object. This is the rebounding of a perfectly elastic cosmos.

This requirement for the fabric of reality to return to equilibrium, to annihilate duality and return to unity, is known as the Law of Equilibrium.

The Law of Equilibrium derives from the need of an elastic cosmos to return to balance. It applies equally to frogs, quarks, planets, individuals, groups, and nations—indeed, to the whole of manifest existence. It operates on all levels, applying equally in physical, emotional, and intellectual contexts, and touches every aspect of our lives. It is the foundation of ethics and the creator of time.

Whenever the fabric of reality is pushed or pulled one way or another, an equal and opposite force is generated. The force that counterbalances will is called karma. Will and karma are a duality: they're dependent on and in opposition to each other, and one cannot exist without the other.

With each and every act of will necessitating a corresponding act of karma, will creates a time line. Will needs a future in which it can be balanced. If you imagine will rippling the fabric of reality, it's the Law of Equilibrium that creates the future in which these ripples return and wash over us. The Law of Equilibrium is the pendulum of the cosmic clock—will pushing the pendulum one way and karma pushing it back, and so the cosmic clock ticks.

As products of will, all actions, emotions, desires, and thoughts must necessarily recoil on their initiator as karma. To initiate a violent act guarantees you the role somewhere, sometime, as its victim. To initiate a hurtful act guarantees you the role somewhere, sometime, as its recipient. To initiate a kindly act guarantees you the role somewhere, sometime, as its beneficiary. With each action, emotion, desire, and thought, you create your future experiences. This is enormously empowering, for it places your future very firmly in your control.

But more than this, the Law of Equilibrium means that it's simply not possible to receive what you've never given. So the principle also applies looking backwards. Your current experiences are the result of what you've done, felt, desired, and thought—in the past. To be a victim of a violent act, or a recipient of a hurtful or a kindly act, is assurance of some measure of participation in like acts somewhere in the chain of lives that comprise your past.

This was a contentious view in the physical world, and it's not much different here. People will defend their belief that their good fortune is "owed them," yet reject the philosophy when they're victims of adversity or crime. They will embrace the concept of karma in relation to creating the future, yet deny it as the creator of the present in any controversial context. People are attracted to the concept of perfect justice, yet consider it offensive when applied to the victims of rape, torture, or genocide. It's an understandable reaction—but you can't have it one way and not the other.

The fact is, no actions are unpunished or unrewarded if your perspective extends far enough into the future, and no condition of birth or life experience is unjust if your perspective extends far enough into the past. When viewed from higher states of consciousness than the astral, in the realms of abstract mind and intuition, this concept is embraced as truth. Free of the distortion of personal feelings and prejudicial thought-forms, the higher mind sees the concept as it is—beautiful, symmetrical, and simply the natural consequence of an elastic cosmos.

But while we can state the principle of perfect justice with absolute certainty, astral consciousness isn't high enough to observe the weaving of cause and effect across lifetimes. And so, from here, we can't see the whole picture. For that kind of view we have to raise our consciousness one or two steps closer to the indivisible reality than we are at present.

However, we do know some of the principles by which karma leapfrogs across lifetimes to land on your back. We know that forces produced in one world need to be balanced in that world, and that karma can only return to wash over us as fast as the matter of the different worlds allows.

Will that translates into physical action will generate physical karma, and will that translates into feelings and lower thoughts will generate astral karma. The generation of karma can occur quickly in the astral world because of the nature of astral matter, which waits for no one, but physical karma is slowed considerably by the sluggishness of physical matter, which ripples like treacle. The consequences of physical actions can take some time to rebound, and they can't wash over you if you're not there. So, physical acts that remain unbalanced at the time of death are held in the indelible memory—the perfect elasticity—of the cosmos, waiting for your next incarnation. It's this memory, or unbalanced will/karma, that's ultimately responsible for sucking you back into the physical world.

Because every action, emotion, desire, and thought recoils on the initiator, the Law of Equilibrium is the foundation and meaning of ethics. Injure your neighbor and you cause yourself suffering of the same nature and the same magnitude. You may as well poke yourself in the eye, shoot yourself in the foot, or create a thoughtform of self-hatred. It's a little-known fact, but the wise do good because they know they're the direct beneficiaries of the good they do others. And that's the best thing of all about the Law of Equilibrium—it removes all distance between a virtuous life and self-interest.

Creating time and ethics, restoring balance, making self-interest and a virtuous life synonymous, reaching across lifetimes and sucking you back into birth—the Law of Equilibrium is responsible for quite a lot. It's also perfectly symmetrical, beautiful, universal, absolute, incontrovertible, and empowering. It empowers you to change your future through the exercise of your will—with absolute confidence in the result.

With love as our compass, and the empowerment of our will, we turn to Nature for our last requirement: wisdom. Nature is the only infallible teacher. She is the keeper of the cupboard of wisdom, and the key to this cupboard is the Law of Correspondences.

The Law of Correspondences

If you stand at the side of a still lake where you can see the trees or mountains of the world above reflected in the water below, you should stop a while and contemplate the words of Hermes Trismegistus: "That which is above is as that which is below, and that which is below is as that which is above."

With those words he stated the Law of Correspondences, or the Law of Analogy or Symmetry, the corollary of "the whole is enfolded in every part." The result of this law is a coherent and organized cosmos where every detail is meaningful, and where remarkable complexity coexists with consistency and simplicity. When you grasp the Law of Correspondences, you grasp the language that nature uses to reveal and instruct.

The Law of Correspondences makes an insight in one context insightful in others; a law in one context a law in others; a design in one system a design in others. Physical laws pop up in the realms of emotion and thought; our chakras are like miniature suns and black holes that we can direct with our will; energy currents in the Earth are mirrored in our bodies; the life cycle of the cosmos is mirrored in the life cycle of a tree; and the water cycle—evaporation, condensation, and precipitation—mirrors the cycle of reincarnation. Symmetries are everywhere, analogy works, and the treasures of the universe can be explored with insight and extrapolation.

Show me a system and I'll show you how and where its design is replicated in immense variations of context and scale. Show me an evolution and I'll show you evolutions along parallel lines. Show me a microcosm and I'll extrapolate from it to deduce the macrocosm. Looking for God? Don't look to the heavens, for heaven's sake—it's much easier and more illuminating to look at yourself. The Law of Correspondences means that you were made in "His" image—you're a microcosm of the universe. In fact, there isn't a single part of your universe that isn't reflected somewhere in the design and function of the universe at large.

"Yeah, sure," you say. "Look, up there in the sky—there's the penile constellation, and over there, the armpit nebula." Very droll, but it's closer to the truth than you think. Because the whole is enfolded in every part, including you, there must exist within you, within your universe, "organs" of function that enable the expression of that whole. All the parts of all of your bodies are repeated in function in the greater world about you—and vice versa.

For example, the functions of your former spleen (the filtration and recycling of blood cells) are reflected in the functions of your solar plexus chakra, and in organs of filtration and recycling of life-force elsewhere in the cosmos. The functions of your old sexual organs are reflected in the functions of your sacral chakra, and in organs of evolutionary progress elsewhere in the cosmos. The functions of your previous nervous system are reflected in your nadis (your current energy pathways), in the energy system of Earth, and in currents of energy elsewhere in the cosmos.

As well as repetition of function, we see repetition of design. The basic design of a nucleus within concentric spheres is repeated at huge intervals of scale as the atom, the human body, the solar system, and the galaxy. The atom consists of a nucleus with orbiting charged clouds. Your astral body consists of a dense core of an identifiable you surrounded by your aura, an ovoid consisting of the swirling clouds of your feelings and thoughts. The solar system consists of a central star with orbiting planets; galaxies consist of a galactic center with orbiting discs or spiral arms. The pattern repeats at scales smaller than the atom and larger than the galaxy. The atom has components of similar design that are as small in relation to it as it is in relation to the solar system; and the universe is made up of a system of galaxies orbiting a universal nucleus, *ad infinitum*, as far as we know.

The design of a nucleus within concentric spheres is a function of the receptive and emissive principles. The receptive principle exists as the curvature of space without which the system couldn't exist. The emissive principle exists as the nuclei, the central portion where you find most of the mass. In the physical world we observed space curving in the presence of a massive object, like the sun. From our perspective here, we see that it's not mass that causes space to curve, but rather curved space that causes mass. Mass is the emissive or convex side of the rubber sheet. On the "other side" you necessarily find the receptive principle, in the form of curved space, literally "pulling" mass into existence.

The receptive and emissive principles could be described as the tools used by cosmic will (reflected as the laws of nature) to create the building blocks of the worlds. Only in the "marriage" of these concepts can conception result, and children be produced. For anything to be created—whether it's a galaxy, a painting, a fungus, or a baby—these principles must come together. You can imagine the two principles as two sides of a triangle, where they meet is coitus, and the third side of the triangle as their "child." And so we move from duality to trinity, and we can unfold another finger. There are many examples of trinities, just as there are many examples of dualities, but the basic one consists of the emissive principle, the receptive principle, and the product of their intercourse.

As well as repetition of function and design, we also see repetition of organization. The organization of the universe is based on the concept of a system of systems. Inside each cell in your physical body were systems for making proteins, transforming energy, reproduction, and transport. These cooperated to form functional cells that cooperated to form tissues such as muscles, organs, and bones. These in turn cooperated to form circulatory, nervous, and digestive systems, which all cooperated to form that wonderful thing you lived in before you died.

Your astral body is similarly a system of systems. Your chakras draw in and transform energy, your nadis direct and channel that energy, and your aura reproduces your feelings and thoughts in objective form. The cosmos is an unimaginably immense system of systems performing all these functions according to the Law of Correspondences. Wherever we look, from the human body to the universe as a whole, we see systems working cooperatively to form other systems, each system replicating its essential function and design.

The Law of Correspondences gives you a little universe all your very own—your training ground, so to speak—and as you prove masterful with your current universe, the process of evolution will unfold new ones.

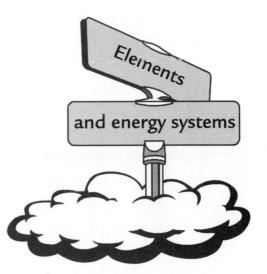

Elements

and energy systems

We began our counting exercise with an Enfolded All projecting the ideals of the cosmos-to-be as a unity. Then, as we raised a second finger, the unity fragmented into a duality, whose intercourse began to manifest the cosmos. So now that we have matter, we can unfold another finger and count to four, because there happen to be four distinct qualities of matter.

They're called the four elements, and together they make things happen—things like combustion, metabolism, perception, energy, and evolution. Ladies and gentlemen, may I present earth, water, air, and fire.

With the essential attributes and interrelationships of their namesakes, these four conditions of matter are the four essential cogs in any manifest process. We'll look at two examples from the physical world first, to show how they combined to make physical things happen. Let's look at how they kept your old body alive and how your physical perception was tied to them.

Metabolism, the process by which your physical body functioned, was a product of the interrelationship of the four elements. Earth was there as the nutrients used for structure and fuel. Water was there as the medium in which all biological processes occurred. Air was there as the materials to combust the fuel, and fire was there as the heat and energy that was produced.

Your perception of the physical world was a function of your brain and its sensory extensions—your eyes, ears, mouth, and nose, and your sense of touch and position. Your sense of touch was designed to orient you to the earth and enable the sensations of feeling and resistance. Your sense of taste and smell were designed to detect substances that were dissolved in water. Hearing was your perception of the vibrations of the air; and sight enabled your perception of objects illuminated by the fire of the sun—light.

The elements are concepts that describe four different states of matter, each with particular properties and predictable relationships. If we identify these properties in the processes around us, we can gain significant insight into them. We can, for example, predict behavior, relationships, and affinities, and the consequences of imbalances.

Like the two physical processes just mentioned—metabolism and perception—the processes of your astral body can also be described as functions of the four elements. Let's take a look at the structure and function of your astral body, and its correlation with the four elements and to the solar system as a whole.

There's a direct connection between the sun and the center of the earth, in a higher dimensional geometry. Energy from the sun reaches the earth in two ways: from within through this connection, and from without through the broad range of energies that reach the earth's surface through space. Stemming from within the connection at Earth's core are channels of force that spiral and thread outward to form our planet's energy network. Where these channels of force run close to the surface, in a manner similar to capillaries, we call them geodetic currents.

Enter the amazing Law of Correspondences, for there's also a connection, in a higher dimensional geometry, between the sun and our bodies. So the energy from the sun reaches us in two ways as well: from within through our solar plexus chakra, via the earth; and from without through the broad range of energies that reach us through space. Stemming from within the connection are channels of force that spiral and thread upwards to form our energy network, mirroring the energy network of the earth. Our channels of force are called nadis, or meridians, and our chakras are the major force centers along their route.

For simplicity, we'll name the chakras according to their approximate physical location. But before we describe our energy system in detail, we should acknowledge our limitations. As our chakras are part of our non-physical bodies, and therefore exist in a different geometry, they don't correspond to any physical location exactly. Different observers can give the same chakra a different physical position. In fact, we face difficulties whenever we use any term relating to "where." Energies that well up from other dimensions are notoriously slippery. The appearance and functionality of our energy system also varies with our degree of development. For example, our nadis may unify as we perfect ourselves. The separate pathways that we generally see would therefore cease to exist. Our chakras, too, can appear as anything from sluggish, unremarkable whirls—right through to flame-throwing supernovas.

Limitations aside, we know quite a lot about the energy that flows within our astral body.

The energy that comes from the sun and reaches us from within is generally referred to as our life force or libido. Yes, we have the sun to thank for that as well. One aspect of this energy is called kundalini, and kundalini has two manifestations: a sustaining warmth and a sleeping fire-breathing dragon. In the physical world the term was usually restricted to the dragon bit, but kundalini has dual roles, just as fire emits both heat and light. The sleeping dragon will awaken naturally at a certain point in our evolution and then proceed to stimulate our chakras into full activity, opening wide the doorways of our unfolding self. This dormant aspect only awakens if its bed is set on fire—and we'll look at how to do that without incinerating ourselves in the process, soon.

Stemming from our base chakra is our major nadi, or energy channel, called Sushumna. Basically following where your old spine used to be, Sushumna connects your base chakra with your crown chakra. It's through your crown chakra that your higher self connects with your different bodies.

Before we continue, we're going to take a small detour, because this concept of higher self is important in our quest to "know thyself."

What we generally think of as "self" is what we call our lower self or personality, but in reality, our personality is only our temporary self for a particular lifetime. It consists of a mental vehicle, an astral vehicle, and a physical vehicle—and so our personality is rather like a three-car garage. Our higher self, or individuality, on the other hand, is the essential self that links our lifetimes. Our individuality expresses itself in successive personalities for the purpose of gaining experience and unfolding its potential.

Separating the concept of self into a higher and a lower self and shifting our identification to the former is vital for our growth and a significant step forward in our quest to "know thyself"—but it's not the whole answer. Our higher self is, although spectacular, almost certainly only another aspect of us. Because the whole is enfolded in every part, the search for the answer to "Who am I?" is a long process, and probably much like opening a very large set of Russian dolls.

It's through your crown chakra that your higher self connects with your personality, and, as you evolve and increasingly identify with your higher self, you begin to recognize that it has quite independent needs. In the process, you gain practice in using your will from this higher perspective, and you begin to rein in your personality to stop it running your life. It's this joyous and difficult process—when undertaken consciously—that's called "entering the path." This is the path of conscious spiritual progress. To walk it we must recognize our connection to the unity, learn to will from the perspective of our higher self, and work as conscious contributors to the progress of evolution.

The path requires that we slay the enemies of lust, anger, greed, delusion, pride, and envy—and that we weed out all selfishness and permutations of hate. It also requires the development, in high degree, of love, wisdom, and strength of will. Much changes in our energy system as these things are accomplished, but the relevant change here is that they make our crown chakra increasingly receptive to a particular range of spiritual energies that are vital for our progress. It is these energies, when drawn down to the base chakra, which set kundalini's bed on fire.

Kundalini is an enormously powerful force. When awakened through self-development and the reception of spiritual energies through our crown chakra, we become sufficiently well developed for its awakening to be a huge leap forward. Kundalini empowers *all* existing qualities, so if you haven't eliminated lust, anger, greed, delusion, pride, and envy, you're in serious trouble. Without the necessary strengths, virtues, and purity, awakened kundalini will very quickly spiral you into a living hell—and that's no joke. The dangers of premature awakening are very real and very serious.

Let's take a closer look now at those wonderful whirlpools of consciousness, those apprentice suns and black holes, those windows on the world we call our chakras.

The word *chakra* is Sanskrit for "wheel,"
and you have seven of these whirlpools of
conscious energy in your body. They function as doorways to particular regions, energies, and experiences, and play a vital
role in our unfolding. To learn how to use
them, we need to know how to activate
them and how to control their emissive
and receptive aspects.

We can use the emissive and receptive
principles with our chakras to open ourselves up to the permutations of love and

close ourselves off to the permutations of hate. As we've seen, a thoughtform's purpose in life is to dock with a host and reproduce itself, and to dock with a host there has to be an affinity. The best and perfect defense against undesirable thoughtforms is to have no affinity with them—in other words, to have no matter in our astral body capable of response. But for the imperfect of us there's a second line of defense. Thoughtforms generated by hate discharge themselves through our solar plexus chakra, but they can only enter when the chakra is receptive. A consciously emissive solar plexus chakra confers a temporary immunity.

Thoughtforms generated by love discharge through our heart chakra. A receptive heart chakra opens us up to these higher and desirable feelings, and stimulates their potential for healing and growth. Master a receptive solar plexus chakra and an emissive throat chakra, for example, and you can sing like an angel. Master a receptive brow chakra and you'll be able to see a whole lot more than you can at present—for the brow chakra is the doorway to the vision of the higher self.

You make a chakra receptive or emissive just as you do everything else: with your will. You just do it (or attempt to do it), watch the results, and practice. Astral matter is easily molded and affected by will.

On the Sushumna highway, between your base chakra and your crown chakra, are five other multidimensional energy centers: in ascending order, they are your sacral chakra, solar plexus chakra, heart chakra, throat chakra, and brow chakra. A helpful way of looking at them is to imagine the cosmos as a rainbow and your chakras as seven windows, each providing a view of a particular band of the rainbow's spectrum. Your base chakra, for example, would be your window on the red wavelengths, your sacral chakra your window on the orange wavelengths, and so on.

Winding in a spiral fashion around Sushumna, from your base chakra to your brow chakra, are the secondary nadis, Ida and Pingala. They work with Sushumna (the primary nadi) in the ascent and descent of energies through our bodies. This arrangement is symbolized by the caduceus, or wand of Hermes, a winged staff with two snakes twining up around it in the form of a double helix.

Our nadis are conduits for a range of energies, all of which ultimately come from the sun: the spiritual energies, which descend through our crown chakra; the kundalini energies, which rise through our base chakra; and prana, which enters through our solar plexus chakra. Prana is part of the broad spectrum of radiation emanating from the sun, and is as vital to sustaining life here as sunshine was in the physical world. Your solar plexus chakra is naturally receptive to prana, as your physical lungs were naturally receptive to air. Much like lungs, your solar plexus chakra draws in prana and distributes it throughout your body.

Prana differs from sunshine in that it's a lot more user-friendly, for it can be directed by the will. In the physical world it was highly responsive to the combination of will and controlled breath, and could be directed to fuel healing processes. Here it can be directed by will to clear stagnant energies and vitalize our astral senses.

Our astral energy system can be compared to a magnet with two poles, with the base chakra representing the pole of matter and the crown chakra representing the pole of spirit. Each chakra represents a level and quality of interaction along the spectrum of spirit-matter, rising from the most material aspects at the base to the most spiritual aspects at the crown. The base, sacral, and solar plexus chakras are referred to as "the three lower chakras." They represent the more material aspects of the spectrum and are predominantly used by our lower self.

Our base chakra is a swirling vortex pointing down to the earth, with which it connects. It is receptive of the earth's energies and emissive of waste products. The base chakra is our anchor to Earth, and its affinity is, unsurprisingly, with the element earth. Both aspects of kundalini rise from here; it's the material pole of our energy magnet, and the material anchor point of our nadis.

When our base chakra is underfunctioning, we feel disconnected to the world and lack the will to survive. When it's overfunctioning, our will to survive overrides all else. In this parlous condition we live an instinctive and selfish life, where Earth's resources are mere commodities for our avarice. When our base chakra is balanced, we experience ourselves as part of nature, feel instinctively that we belong in the world, and are respectful of Earth and its resources.

Our sacral chakra is our connection to the unconscious mind, and its affinity is with the element water. Here we find the will to reproduce, sexual desires, and the personal aspects of imagination and interpersonal love.

When our sacral chakra is overfunctioning, we think with our genitals. Unfortunately, they're notoriously poor thinkers. When this chakra is underfunctioning, we find ourselves fearful of personal intimacy and of opening up our unconscious mind. We'll cover balancing our sexual energy soon.

Our sacral chakra can very easily draw from the vast sea of sexual imagery in the collective unconscious. Unrestrained, this powerful imagery can hijack our will and take control of our steering wheel. It then proceeds to drive us around like a maniacal, oversexed taxi driver, and the fare (the consequences of this) can be very expensive. When the emissive (masculine) aspect of sexual energy is unrestrained, we indiscriminately dissipate (or "ejaculate" when in the physical world) an exceptionally precious energy source, and dry up like old prunes. Every time a male ejaculates, he loses vitality. Each ejaculation diverts energy from other processes to replenishing the stocks, and the cost of replenishment is high. When the losses are excessive, the costs materialize as physical and mental weakness, and premature ageing. When the receptive (feminine) aspect of sexual energy is unrestrained, we indiscriminately absorb the most intimate of energies from people we wouldn't share bathwater with in our right mind.

Our solar plexus chakra is where we find our sense of personal self—that is, the way our personality expresses itself. Our solar plexus chakra is naturally receptive to prana—it absorbs it, filters it, and distributes it as automatically as we used to breathe. Its emissive aspect is the home of our personal sun, radiating our sense of personal self, but although we refer to it this way, in relative terms it's a mere hot water bottle compared with the real fire of the higher chakras. This chakra's affinity is with the element air when it's receptive, and fire when it's emissive.

When our solar plexus chakra is underfunctioning, we're easily manipulated by fear, we look outside of ourselves for identity, live through others, and are particularly vulnerable to the charismatic. Overfunctioning may be displayed as vanity, willfulness, megalomania, and other permutations of self-obsession. When this chakra is balanced, though, it brings a healthy personal self-image and charisma, with none of the permutations of hatred (such as arrogance). It is then that we radiate the positive empowerment of a confident "I am me and I am no one else." However, without the wiser and growing influence of the higher chakras, a powerful solar plexus chakra allows the self-absorbed personality to dominate and draws down the shutters on the bigger, wider world.

Many people—principally our younger brothers and sisters (in an evolutionary sense) and our materially entrenched peers—operate almost wholly through these three lower chakras. Four splendiferous higher centers of consciousness await them, but before we explore them, we need to look at the dragon that is sexual energy.

Dragons and supernovas

Sexual energy is an immensely potent force that wells up continually from within us, and its function is to propel the course of evolution. It's not a force you can stand against—it's been propelling evolution for millennia, and you're not going to stop it. So it can't be repressed, but neither can it be allowed to run wild. Dam it up and it will build and break through at our weakest point. Let it run wild and it will weaken and enslave us. Both of these outcomes are certainties. Sexual energy is not a dragon we can kill, nor is it a dragon we can allow to run amok; fortunately, though, it is a dragon we can tame.

If, at the death of your physical body, you were operating in high gear from your sacral chakra, you face two problems. The first is that you have no way of realizing the physical sensations; you can drink in the energies of others, and you can exist within your fantasies, but you haven't got the gear any more to feel the friction. Like an alcoholic trapped at a Mormon birthday party, you'll be opening every cupboard with increasing desperation, searching for cough mixture, vanilla essence, or mineral turpentine. Add to this the fact that emotions and desires are experienced far more powerfully here, and you may have some idea of what you'll face.

Throughout your physical lifetime, your desires were molding the astral matter around you according to the nature of your lower mind. So the second situation you face is that you're surrounded by the creations of your sexual imagery. Here, in their element, powered by the years or decades of thought you put into them, they're beyond your control and they replay themselves incessantly.

There are a number of drawbacks to this nonstop sex video in six dimensions. First, we're fuelling desires that we simply cannot realize in the form the images depict. Second, the imagery is so powerful and constant that it can completely dominate our astral life, effectively excluding us from all else. Third, that which was private in the physical world is rarely as attractive out in the open; and fourth, its relentlessness is guaranteed to outlive our tolerance. The consequence of all this is that it becomes a constant and unavoidable reminder of our weaknesses. This is a common experience in the astral world, and while it can be long-lived, it can't last longer than the batteries we powered it with. But there would hardly be a soul who, in their past or future lives, hasn't or won't experience this and subsequently resolve to control it.

To balance our sacral chakra requires knowledge and, like everything else, the application of will. The way to tame this dragon is to conserve it, channel it, and transform it. This involves controlling the emissive nature of our masculine energies and the receptive nature of our feminine energies.

We all have both male and female sexual energies within us, irrespective of our gender. Our evolutionary path requires us to develop and balance these energies. Our sexual orientation is the external reflection of this internal process. The pursuit of either one sex or the other in the exterior world means we need to develop that aspect, at that time, within us.

This subject is of vital importance because we cannot make evolutionary progress without understanding and mastering our sexual energies. Most of the problems we encounter arise from an undisciplined imagination. So if we employ our will to restrain our imagination, we can eradicate many sexual problems at their source.

The conservation of male sexual energy in the physical world requires conservation of the ejaculate; in the astral world it requires controlling the emissive aspect of our sacral chakra. An uncontrolled emissive sacral chakra creates uncontrollable sexual imagery and drags out the consequences just described.

Being generally more emissive in nature, the issue with the male aspect of sexual energy is giving in general, not so much who we give it to. Being generally more receptive in nature, the issue with the female aspect of sexual energy is not receiving as such, but who we receive it from. Our feminine aspect is highly sus-

ceptible to the harmful energies of weak or selfish partners. Consequently, learning who to love, and choosing
our sexual partners with the greatest of care, is of the
utmost importance. An uncontrolled receptive sacral
chakra is just as dumb and dangerous as uncontrolled
reception into any orifice, anywhere.

Sexual energy is like fire: it generates both heat and
light. Many of us have only experienced it as heat, but
sexual energy can be seen in a far greater context, with
heat as the lowest and least of its powers. As we learn to
control our sexual energy, we become stronger physically, emotionally, and mentally, and this enables us to
channel our sexual energies into other areas. Sexual energy is a limitless power supply that we can use to fuel
any activity, be it creativity, meditation, study, moral
strength, or spiritual progress. Like everything else, sexual energy is neither intrinsically good nor bad—it's
what we do with it that makes it so. If we can learn to
conserve the dragon and gradually let it build, while
working on improving the receptive nature of our
crown chakra, we will find that we can draw this immense power up into our higher chakras and increase
their emissive and receptive capacity enormously.

Let's take a look at the four higher chakras: the heart, throat, brow, and crown. These are the windows of consciousness through which our higher self interacts with our lower self—and with the cosmos at large. The four higher chakras come increasingly into play as our evolution proceeds, and there's an inverse relationship between their development and our reliance on our lower chakras.

As we increase our usage of our heart chakra, we reduce our reliance on our solar plexus chakra. As we increase our usage of our throat chakra, we reduce our reliance on our sacral chakra; and as we increase our usage of our brow chakra, we reduce our reliance on our base chakra. This transfer from our lower chakras to our higher chakras is the prelude to the caterpillar-to-butterfly-like emergence of our higher self.

Within our heart chakra resides the will to love, but this love, unlike the personal love of the solar plexus chakra, is spiritual love. This is the shining heart of the saint and the wisdom of the poet. As the heart chakra awakens, our feelings change. They change from being selfish and narrowly focused to being expansive and spiritual. When it really gets going, it bestows the ability to instinctively understand the feelings of all other astral entities, it enhances our capacity to direct prana, and it lights up our corner of the world with the beautiful, unifying, and necessary power of unselfish love. The heart chakra's affinity is with the element of water. Overfunctioning isn't a problem with any of the higher chakras—as if you can have too much unselfish love!

Within our throat chakra resides the will to do. Here lies the power to make things happen: to materialize resources, to pay attention, to hear, to communicate, to encourage green buds to open with our inspiration and power. The throat chakra's affinity is with the element Air, and as it awakens, so does our capacity to hear the needs of our brothers and sisters and inspire them with the strength and breadth of our vision. As our throat chakra awakens, our reliance on our solar plexus chakra decreases, for we actually begin to generate our own prana. The throat chakra is distinguished by the power of high and unselfish oratory, totally devoid of the slightest self-aggrandizement. When it really gets going, it enables us to help our brothers and sisters through our ability to know their past, present, and future.

Our brow chakra is the eye of our intuitive mind, the will to know. Here is the doorway to wisdom, for it's through this center of consciousness that we obtain direct knowledge. This is the kind of knowledge that doesn't come from books, nor from the mouths of the wisest of teachers—it comes by actually being there, or being it, and knowing it from the inside. The brow chakra is our window on the transcendent perspective of our higher self, and its affinity is with the element of fire. As our brow chakra awakens, our reliance on our base chakra decreases, eventually enabling us to break free of the anchor that binds us to Earth.

Our crown chakra is our doorway to consciousness beyond our higher self. There goes another Russian doll! Its main role, at our stage of evolution, is the reception of spiritual energies to stimulate the awakening of the other higher chakras. The full awakening of the crown chakra denotes the perfection of human faculties, the crowning achievement in the line of human evolution. This is spiritual realization, a return to the Source, the Unity from which we arise, our ticket to pure unencumbered consciousness. This is no mere window or doorway—the crown chakra is the supernova of enlightenment, and the reason many statues of Buddha show flames leaping out of the top of his head.

This world, the astral world, isn't the end of the line. It's only a pit stop on life's highway—a pit stop that may take from a few hours to a few centuries, but a pit stop nonetheless. Vastly superior states of consciousness exist. They can be fully experienced through the awakening of our higher chakras, or experienced—to our current capacity—through death. So as good as the astral world can be, the quicker we pass through it, the better.

It's time now to pull out the largest-scale map we can find, describe the whole of the cycle of reincarnation, and look as far beyond the astral world as we can.

The Ferris wheel of life

Birth and death are transition points as life moves from one state to another. They're like the point of intersection between any fragmented phenomena: the point at which matter becomes energy, a particle becomes a wave, magnetism becomes electricity, or Trinidad becomes Tobago. We cross these points a number of times as our lives cycle through the realms of nature. This is the Ferris wheel in the amusement park of life, the cycle of reincarnation.

It's also my favorite part of our tour, because we're about to take a virtual ride. We're going to hop on for one revolution, one dip into and out of matter, one "lifetime" in the broader sense of the word.

So, here's your ticket—hop on, and hold onto this glass of water for me.

You're sitting in a carriage at the bottom of the Ferris wheel, in a physical body, holding on to a glass of water and wondering why. As you look at the water you notice that it's not moving—it has turned to ice. "Ah, this must be the solid world," you say, pleased at having worked out the analogy. Here, in this cramped geometry, you're much like water constrained in the form of ice.

As the carriage moves forward, you see in the foreground a vast array of different physical life forms, and in the background you see a high wall. You're not high enough yet to see beyond this wall; this is the limit of your physical perception. As the Ferris wheel slowly rotates, you experience the joys and sufferings of physical life. Your suffering is the result of thinking you're a Volvo and behaving that way, craving fuel and new dashboard ornaments while the real you starves. And so your physical life is lived—the personality craves, the higher self goes hungry, and you spend your time exercising your will satisfying something you're not. And all this exercising of your will pushes and pulls at the fabric of reality and creates your karma.

Although the Ferris wheel turns slowly, it generally turns too fast for the karmic pendulum, so death may whisk you away before the consequences of your actions can swing back at you. And so your ledger, in terms of the Law of Equilibrium, can carry significant levels of debt.

Then, suddenly, a pterodactyl swoops from the sky and plucks your body from the carriage. Flipping you around so that you're pointing down its gullet, it tosses its head and swallows you in mid-flight. You watch, shocked and surprised to be still watching from your carriage. "That must have been the point of death," you say. And it wasn't so bad, really. You survived, and the gruesome bit didn't seem to actually happen to you—it just happened to your body.

So now you're sitting in the carriage in your astral body, and the glass of ice is no longer in your hand. You see that the bottom of the carriage is wet, and you realize you must have dropped the glass when the lizard got you. "This must be the liquid world," you say, again catching on quickly, "and the point of death was the melting point." You feel very different now, far less constrained, far more mobile, and far more able to express yourself, much as ice would when suddenly liberated in the form of water.

Having risen farther from the ground, you can now see beyond the high wall. At the base of the Ferris wheel you see the fluid bodies of those you knew before you melted. "Don't worry," you call out, "I survived the reptile attack!" But you're too high, and they can't hear you. The array of life here is far greater than anything you've seen before, and the air pulses with the color and form of every feeling, emotion, and desire.

As the Ferris wheel rolls on, your astral body reorganizes and you experience the joys and sufferings of astral life. Your suffering is the result of your desires for useless things (as far as your higher self is concerned), and the consequence of your inner reality externalizing. You're surrounded by a lifetime of feelings and the collective thoughtforms of your culture. If the majority of people in your community believed that after death you'd be met by the Three-Headed Goat God of Thebes—well, there he is! There's so much that's beautiful, so much that's ridiculous, and so much that's ugly, much like the physical world—and you live it according to your character and your ability to see beyond the creations of the ignorant.

Still, there's also lots of joy here, especially for those who are relatively unshackled by ignorance and the permutations of hatred. You could take a guided tour such as this, or maybe see a post-death counselor. Or, for fun, you could zoom to the pterodactyl's nest and watch as bits of you are regurgitated into hungry young mouths.

And so your astral life is lived. Your experiences improve as the lowest materials of your astral body gradually dissipate, until finally the finer aspects of the realm open to you according to your highest emotional development.

Meanwhile, the Ferris wheel has been turning, and just as you're beginning to really enjoy this place, you notice the water at the bottom of the carriage is evaporating. "Uh-oh, not again!" you say. "Looks like the boiling point and another transition," and you're quite right. The world around you fades, and . . . that's it! All pretty boring, actually, compared with your last death. You're vaguely aware of your astral corpse floating away on an astral current. Like an old piece of furniture left out for garbage collection, it attracts the attention of a mischievous nature spirit, who decides to borrow it. He's probably going to impersonate you and shock your astral friends or appear at some séance or something—but what can you do?

You're sitting in the carriage, in a body made of mind-stuff, with the last of the water at the bottom of the carriage turning to steam. Welcome to the gaseous world. Your first impression is an overwhelming sensation of bliss, and a feeling of enormous vitality. You feel so free—you feel virtually limitless—and you can express yourself by direct thought, with no barrier of language and no possibility of misunderstanding. This is all the joy, freedom, and capacity of the astral world raised to the power of a gazillion, minus all the grubby bits. And up here, near the top of the Ferris wheel, the breadth of view is enormous. It feels as if you can see the whole world. And forget zooming, because you can now zap, and zapping is even more fun and much more efficient. Point A to point B now has no intervening space— thanks to an even less restricted geometry.

The thoughtforms here are huge, multidimensional, majestic, and amazing—some are like whole worlds—and all are indescribably beautiful. This rarefied matter only responds to the highest of ideals and conceptual thought, so all personal thoughtforms have been left behind. And then you realize that the inside-out process that started with your first death and externalized your lower mind has now externalized your higher mind. This is the realm where the higher mind—yours and everyone else's, including that of the cosmos—is at home.

This is where you live your "heaven life." With all personal desires, selfishness, and permutations of hatred worn away before you can enter, this is Heaven indeed. None of those things can be experienced here. The only parts of your astral life that carry over are the seeds of your emotional development, which lie dormant until the Ferris wheel takes you back down.

Your body looks and feels as if it's made of dense mist, and you can see the misty bodies of those who are conscious in the astral and physical realms. But while your astral body was familiar because you functioned in it each time you slept, your body of mind-stuff takes a little longer to get used to. It's a body that for most of us is still far from fully developed, and, as in both the worlds you previously inhabited, you're limited by the extent to which you have developed your powers of perception.

You experience the heaven world in ways that correspond to your level of intellectual and spiritual development. If there's been little love, generosity, unselfishness, and higher thought in your life so far, Heaven will be bliss, but only a fraction of what it is to someone more advanced. You observe and participate in the heaven world through windows of self-development. The least of these windows is created by unselfish family affection. Another, better window is created by religious devotion. Better still is the window created by devotion expressing itself in work. Even more light enters windows created by unselfish pursuits in spiritual, philosophical, scientific, literary, and artistic arenas, and windows created by service to humanity. Although the infinite ocean of the cosmic mind exists in the heaven world, your capacity to appreciate it ranges from literally being the whole of it to dipping only a toe in it. Still, even that much will humble you with its scope and beauty.

Here, you're unimaginably closer to all you love. You relate to them on a higher level than you did in physical or astral life, so it doesn't matter whether they're currently in a physical body or not. In this world, matter responds instantly to every thought, so we can't say there are no clouds or harps, because if you want them, you've got them. But it's only clouds and harps if that's your thing. Heaven is the ultimate in the fulfillment of all your higher thoughts, so for each of us it's different. It is instant, simultaneous, unimaginable contact with all those you love and the best views possible through all the windows you've created.

But nothing lasts forever, and there's something higher even than Heaven. We only call Heaven "Heaven" because it's the highest level most of us attain with a reasonable level of consciousness.

Eventually the mist begins to clear, its temperature rising to the point where its molecules start to break apart. Sounds like another transition. Yes, it's another death, but the last for a while, because now you're at the very top of the Ferris wheel. Here, the view is beyond description. It's hard to appreciate the view, though, because at our present stage of development we feel giddy and faint at these heights. But this is our real home, the home of our soul, which is higher than that of mind. This is the home of our intuition. It's all the joy, freedom, and capacity of the heaven world raised to the power of a gazillion, but without any of the windows. No such limitations exist.

The seeds of your emotional development are still in your pocket, but added to them now are the seeds of your intellectual development. You'll need this packet of seeds when you start running out of oxygen and feel the need to come back down, which will probably be quite soon. Before you go, though, some truths imprint themselves on your consciousness. As you live and move through the realms, all the highest qualities and capacities you unfold are stored here, in the home of your soul, permanently. This is a deposit-only account, so little by little—or lot by lot—you increase your ability to function in this exalted world. This is the level at which an adept has a commanding consciousness. Your admiration for those who have achieved this goal is immense, as is your gratitude to them for showing the way. You understand this pinnacle of human evolution as your destiny. This is where your evolution is taking you—and where it will surely deliver you. The only thing that's within your control is how long it will take for you to arrive.

Alas, a sort of harmless equivalent of altitude sickness sets in, and you feel the need to come down. Three things work to make this happen. First, the Law of

Equilibrium. Every act of personal will that remains unbalanced by karma guarantees you a return seat even if you have to sit on someone's lap; you must return for the consequences of your actions. Second, Volvos only feel truly alive with their tires gripping the road, so desire for physical sensation also draws you back down. And third, your intuition is imprinted with the need to do better, so your higher self actually *wants* to return to build further qualities into your soul—qualities that can only be won through the resistance of matter—and to shrug off the heavy weight of your karma.

The Ferris wheel rotates and your focus of consciousness descends. The seeds holding your intellectual development germinate in the steam, and though your soul remains accessible through intuition, around it a new mind is created. As the Ferris wheel continues to cycle, your focus of consciousness dips into the fluid world. The seeds holding your emotional development germinate in the water, and a new body of feeling, emotion, and desire—your astral body—is created around your new mind. Your carriage continues to descend until finally you're pulled into the physical world by strong hands in rubber gloves. You're just bursting to tell the world about the most amazing trip you just had and the amazing things you saw, but your mouth is full of warm nipple and the sweet trickle of life flowing down your throat fills your world completely.

Everything that exists or has ever existed, everything that happens or has ever happened, started as a picture in the medium of mind. Wherever you behold any type of organization of any type of matter, you behold the realization of thought. Thought is the formative energy in the cosmos.

Not only does it build, guide, and determine the workings of the cosmos, but this same power within each and every one of us guides and determines our personal existence. And if that's not a scary thought, it should be. An ill-disciplined mind will drag you around like a rogue elephant—and it's you who pays for the damage. Fortunately, as well as an elephant, we have an elephant-stick called will, and with persistence, will can control even the most belligerent pachyderm.

To properly understand thought, we should really be focused in the heaven world, the home of its highest expressions, and watch it at work within the wonderfully free geometry of that realm. But unless you're prepared to wait around for your next death, you'll have to make do with a brief, dimensionally reduced version of it now.

Every thought creates a form with a job to do. It may be an image of lust, an apparition of dread, or the ideals of a community in harmony, but it will find expression in either mental or astral matter, or a combination of both.

Thoughts that are directed toward material goals, or that contain an emotional or personal quality, find expression in the astral world. Grand ideas, thoughts that rise beyond the selfish and mundane, find expression in the matter of the mental realm. Think the thought "I want to be famous" and watch it form before you in the astral world as objective reality. Now, think the thought "The soul is a seed from God" and watch, and wait, and watch—as nothing happens at all, because even astral matter's too stodgy to realize a thought like that. And so it remains as inner reality. But it has been realized, without doubt, beyond your perceptual reach, in the mental realm, or Heaven. Similarly, if I were to conceptualize "the square root of three," you could no more see it than when you had physical eyes. But in the mental realm, "the square root of three" is a multidimensional, living structure reminiscent of Escher's ascending and descending staircase. Likewise, "abstract" conceptions such as "harmony," "democracy," and "tolerance" also find expression in the mental realm as cohesive structures that are every bit as real and objective as you and me.

The atmosphere is populated and polluted with our thoughtforms—and those of our community and nation—and so we're continually bombarded with a myriad of thoughts and feelings, but the majority of them are mundane and vague. Most of us think the way we do because large numbers of others think that way. Likewise, the "agenda" of thought is strongly influenced by the thoughts already existing. The nature of this thought-geography means that we're not responsible for all the thoughts that come into our mind—however, we are responsible for any we seize, dwell on, invigorate, and send back out. We should aim, of course, to feel our own feelings and think our own thoughts, not someone else's. So, we have to be good at discriminating—adopting only the feelings and thoughts we want and dismissing the rest. Think of it as a buffet—just because it's there doesn't mean you have to eat it, and just because you're there doesn't mean you can't eat somewhere else.

All thought, wherever it first manifests, whether in the mental or astral realm, tends to translate "downward" into more material realms. So thoughts will tend to find some reflection in an emotional context and both will tend to find some reflection in a physical context. But something in the heaven world reflecting into the astral world has to squeeze into a geometry of fewer dimensions, be built of coarser matter, and compete with astral things. Similarly, something in the astral world reflecting into the physical world has to squeeze into a geometry of fewer dimensions again, be built of coarser matter still, and compete with physical things. So the results may take time and they must by definition be debased, but they'll be there, in form or action, somehow, due to the Law of Correspondences. You just have to know where to look and how to interpret it.

How thought translates "down" through the realms is, in general terms, not a mystery. Imagine a horizontal pane of glass on which you sprinkle some fine sand. Now, conjure up a violin bow, hold it vertically, and draw it across the glass. The vibrations cause the particles of sand to assume a form, its nature depending on the character of the vibration and its force. Thought realizes itself in form in the same way. If you imagine the glass and sand as a two-dimensional structure (flat, with no height) and the bow as the appearance of an additional dimension, we have the *modus operandi* of the translation of thought: vibrations originating from higher dimensions organize responsive matter in lower dimensions into representative forms.

What this thought geography does is create a context of inevitability. Thought creates the furrows along which action will inevitably run. This is how free will and fate coexist. Imagine action as water and fate as the geography created by the landscape of thought. You can't change how action flows—it simply follows the geography—but you can change the geography, the thought-landscape over which it flows, and thereby change the events that unfold. In other words, show me the thought geography and I'll tell you the future, and if the thought geography doesn't change in the interim, there's no way I'm going to be wrong.

With the whole of your existence guided and determined by the pictures in your mind, the importance of using thought wisely and skillfully is self-evident. Thought is a tool with which you create your existence, and so, like all good tools, you need to be able to pick it up and put it down and choose and use it like a set of spanners. One way to use thought as a tool is to consciously create thoughtforms for specific purposes, such as to protect, calm, or heal. We'll take a look now at two popular and effective thoughtforms—"The Ice Pick of Love" and "The Disgorging Power-Balloon."

To begin, you need someone to send your thought-form to, so think of someone in need of some hope, joy, and light in their life. Come on now, there must be someone! Now imagine a serious-looking ice-pick of hard, gleaming metal, perfectly designed for cracking the most resilient of matter. Wholly infuse it with the exquisite rose hue of the purest and highest love you can imagine, and there you have it. Think of your friend, tell the ice pick to go, and it's already there, cracking the hard, grey crust of depression and helping the light shine in. Don't agonize over the image; with a little practice you'll simply form it like a snapshot, tell it where to go, and the laws of nature will ensure it does exactly as you intend.

The Disgorging Power-Balloon is a thoughtform whose job it is to swell up with whatever force or quality you fill it with, go to your friend, and disgorge itself into their aura. In the same simple way that you would have picked up the "unleaded" or "diesel" nozzle at a gas station, pick up the nozzle of "health," "moral strength," "peace," or whatever you choose, feel that quality, and stick the nozzle between the power-balloon's lips. The power-balloon is filled in about a second, at which point the nozzle turns off, the power-balloon closes its mouth without a drop being spilled, winks at you, and is gone. As all thoughtforms live to serve, it's already at its destination, disgorging itself and invigorating your friend—even as you return the nozzle to the pump.

You can use these and a myriad other thoughtforms as tools to help those in need. Whenever your thought-forms are motivated by selfishness, they'll remain visible in the astral world. If they're unselfish, they'll disappear and do their job in the heaven world. We should strive to keep our thoughtforms out of the astral world by keeping self-interest at bay, for two reasons. First, because it's good for us, and second, because if your friend has astral consciousness, a disgorging power-balloon homing in on you with its eyes bulging and cheeks fit to burst is *not* a pretty sight.

To form beneficial thought landscapes, you have to learn to control your mind. First, you must put it in its place. It's not you; it's a vehicle of consciousness and a tool. Second, if you imagine your mind as a window, it will only be an effective one if the glass is clear and still. It can't be colored by prejudice, and it can't latch on to every passing thoughtform in the mental atmosphere. The way to clear and still your mind is through meditation.

It's said that as food is to the physical life, so meditation is to the spiritual life. It's through meditation that our vehicles of consciousness calm, come under our will, and learn to respond to higher and higher vibrations. Each effort we make helps thin the veil that divides us from the higher worlds, and brings us closer to the faculty of direct knowledge.

To continue the analogy of mind as a window, we also have to point it in the right direction if we want to fill it with the right things—that is, see the views we want to see. An important way to do this is to look for the desirable qualities—rather than the undesirable ones—in everyone. By practicing this we encourage our mind to admire and appreciate rather than suspect and criticize. The common approach—of looking for the worst in everyone and seizing on their weaknesses while ignoring all that's good—creates one of the most harmful thought geographies, the inevitable consequences of which are various forms of war and disease.

Your imagination is a powerful tool—a wonderful one if you know what you're doing, and a very dangerous one if you don't. Imagine yourself in possession of a quality and you're well on your way to having it, for what you think, you become. Agonize over your excesses, though, and you'll never be rid of them; dwell on your faults and you'll only exacerbate them; berate yourself for your weaknesses and you only enhance their capacity to enslave you. Can you see a pattern?

If you want to improve, don't brood over your faults. Don't think about them. Thought empowers whatever it's directed toward. To have the immense power of the realization of thought on your side, you have to concentrate on developing the virtue opposite to the fault or weakness that you are now, hopefully, going to ignore. So if your weakness is that you take everything to excess, ignore it. Instead, concentrate on and imagine yourself as moderate in all things. If your weakness is that you bristle at the slightest annoyance, ignore it and, instead, concentrate on and imagine yourself as calm and tolerant. Whatever you turn your mind to, realization inevitably follows.

So tell me, who assumed that the elephant-stick was meant to hit the elephant when he misbehaved? No no no, it's not for that at all. His hide is far too thick, and that would be turning the mind to what you wanted to eliminate—and that will never work. The elephant-stick is for throwing in the direction you want the elephant to go—to direct your mind to what you want to create, be, or do—because this elephant is programmed to fetch.

Affinity

and intuition

We've seen how thought creates the landscape along which action must follow. It therefore creates inevitable direction, but things such as people and environments have to come together to build the context in which these events can occur. Riding sidecar to the power of thought is the Law of Affinity, the mechanism by which all these strands come together.

The Law of Affinity makes each and every wavelength seek and attach itself to identical ones. In the physical world, it was called resonance. The wavelengths you generate with your thoughts and feelings create forces of attraction. These reach through the worlds like long, perfectly elastic strands and attach to regions and entities that think and feel in the same way. The Law of Affinity builds the theater in which your thoughts can act.

If you want to attract something to you, you must first summon it from within. Through the Law of Affinity, it will then be inevitably drawn to you from without. The Law of Affinity makes everything possible with perseverance. It's an enabling and empowering law that gives you the power to create destiny. Thought forms the mental landscape, creates the direction for things to happen, and the Law of Affinity brings the parties together so they can. To know and use these laws consciously is to be able to realize absolutely anything you will to do.

If you summon within yourself the vibrations of selfishness, violence, jealousy, or greed, you draw toward you the circumstances in which these things will play themselves out. Similarly, if you summon within yourself higher values, such as the desire to ease suffering, raise awareness, or promote tolerance, then the circumstances in which these things can be realized will be drawn toward you with the same inevitability. Such is the power of the mind.

But just as there are worlds beyond Heaven, there are greater tools than mind. Mind is an excellent tool for analysis—seeing differences and dissecting experiences— but an inadequate tool for synthesis—understanding relationships, seeing unity, and creating new paradigms.

And so you need different tools for different jobs. If you want to chop something up, use an axe; if you want analysis, use your mind. But if you want to put something together, be it a widget, an emotional truth, or two concepts, you need a different tool. For synthesis, you need intuition. Analysis produces knowledge, but synthesis produces insight, and the greatest advances are products of insight.

If you look at the hazards information has to survive before it can reach your consciousness, it's just as well there are other and better tools than mind. First of all, your senses can only gather limited streams of information. Into these narrow rivulets you then throw buckets of dye—coloring them with emotion. The colored rivulets then pour over your established personal and cultural thought-landscape, your shared and accepted patterns, your paradigms or agreements—and these are harsh filters. They define what is real, possible, or meaningful by what they let through—and what is unreal, impossible, or meaningless by what they block out. It's hardly surprising that the runoff from all this can't satisfy your thirst.

Fortunately, the illumination of intuition takes a completely different route, avoiding all these hazards. While sensory input comes from without, intuition comes from within. This is its unique perceptual advantage. The intuitive world, the home of your soul or higher self, at the top of the Ferris wheel, exists in an even less restricted geometry than mind. With the freedom this conveys, you can actually merge your consciousness with the object of your attention, so that subject and object become one. This is the direct knowledge we spoke of before—the faculty of consciousness awakened through our brow chakra.

Imagine being able to merge your consciousness with something or someone around you. Now deepen the image so that your consciousness also merges with every system within that something or someone, and then with every system within that—your attention able to move from one to the other with ease. Now expand this so that your consciousness merges not with just one something or someone, but with every system within every system of everything and everyone around you, simultaneously. As long as your mind hasn't seized up or exploded, you just got a glimpse of the depth and breadth of consciousness in the intuitive world, the world at the very top of the Ferris wheel.

Coming back down for a moment, one of the problems we imperfect humans face—before the faculty of intuition is properly opened up—is differentiating intuition from something else that wafts in. How, for example, can we distinguish an intuition from a prejudice? Fortunately there's a set of criteria: Intuition has no aspect of personal gain, it becomes clearer and stronger with time, and it clarifies in meditation.

Intuition doesn't have to be developed so much as listened for. It's always there, in the background, ready to speak when called on. But it's rarely heard over the incessant chattering and attention seeking of our senses, feelings, and mind. It's through meditation that we learn to control and quieten these naughty vehicles of consciousness. Only then, when they learn to behave, can the sweet song of our intuition be heard.

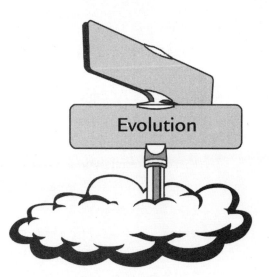

It's hard to imagine a bigger subject than evolution, because it's hard to think of anything that it doesn't include. It's been called "the process that includes all other processes," but it is, essentially, a process of unfolding—bringing potentials into existence. With this kind of scope, much of the subject is beyond our intellectual reach—but fortunately we know bits and pieces.

To help explain some of the bigger bits, we're going to refer to a little book called

The Beginner's Guide to Staging a Play—it's not difficult to imagine evolution as a drama played out on the cosmic stage.

It says, "To stage your play, you need three things. You need a theater as the context in which the play will happen and as the storehouse of your materials; from these materials you'll need to make props and costumes as the visual apparel of the play; and then, you need actors to inhabit the costumes and play out the drama."

Over the page, there's a flow diagram. It shows three paths diverging from this point. The first is for people who have everything and are ready to roll. The next is for people who have nothing as yet—but lots of cash; and the third path is for people who are broke but very patient—and that's us. It says, "This is the most difficult but ultimately the most rewarding route; however, you can give up now unless your raw materials are alive and you're committed for the long haul. Nothing can happen without a basic form of 'aliveness,' and it's going to take much longer than you think. In fact, you'll need aeons"—and then comes the good bit—"because everything you need is going to have to evolve."

In the chapter on evolution, it tells us the kind of "alive" we need. It says, "There are two requirements: your raw materials must be self-organizing and they must have an inherent desire for richness of experience.

"But with that," it says confidently, "you can stage *Aida*."

Continuing, it says, "With self-organization and a desire for richness of experience, you can evolve all the materials you need. With these attributes, your raw materials will express themselves in myriad ways, then work these expressions into ever more workable and complex combinations, which will, in turn, express themselves in myriad ways, and so on. With time, you'll have stable and adaptable building blocks organizing themselves into stable and adaptable structures. Blink an aeon and you'll have a magnificent theater with a storehouse stacked high with an array of versatile materials.

"Blink another aeon and the more advanced of your materials will have evolved feelings—the basic forces of attraction and repulsion will have developed into likes and dislikes. Knowledge will arise from the desire to repeat the pleasant sensations and avoid the unpleasant ones. By this time, some of your materials will be sufficiently useful to deserve the title of 'prop,' and you'll soon find them interacting with other props and putting on costumes in sympathy with their likes and dislikes.

"Meanwhile, within the materials and props, the ability to act is continuing to develop and express itself. From humble beginnings of self-organization and the desire for richness of experience, your props will develop into fledgling actors able to manipulate the matter and forms around them, and this quickens the pace of evolution. The evolution of your young actors accelerates with their experiences in manipulating their environment; and the evolution of the matter and props accelerates by being manipulated, adding organization from without to organization from within. With time, you'll have self-conscious actors capable of sophisticated interaction and communication. Blink an aeon and they'll be throwing tantrums and getting laryngitis on opening night!"

Okay—there's no such book, but it does illustrate the principles at work. For instance, it illustrates the fact that evolution is a living process. Whether it's the subtle matter in the mental realm with its instinctive response to thought, or the densest minerals in the physical world—everything in the cosmos is alive. Life doesn't mysteriously enter the system at the plant stage.

It also illustrates the fact that evolution has three strands. There's the evolution of matter (the materials), the evolution of form (the props and costumes), and the evolution of consciousness (the ability to act).

Consciousness was always there—present from the beginning as the "aliveness" of the raw materials—and it was consciousness that drove the process. It was consciousness within the materials that developed the materials, eventually forming them into props and costumes; and it was consciousness that used the props and costumes as its outer garments to stage the drama.

We can picture something of the organization of the evolutionary process by imagining the three strands of evolution arranged with the strand of consciousness as the core, and with the strands of matter and form winding around it. The evolution of matter and form are the outer and obvious bits—but if that's all you see, you'll miss the point of the whole process, because while we only know bits and pieces about evolution, we're pretty sure we know its point, its essential purpose: the unfolding of consciousness.

We also know the direction the different strands are heading. The outer strands, the evolution of matter and form, flow only one way—into the sensations of matter. The evolution of consciousness, on the other hand—the inner strand—flows in two directions. It is an intrinsic part of the evolution of matter and form, but at its most material expression in the mineral kingdom, having achieved the ultimate in material sensations, it about-turns and flows in the opposite direction as self-consciousness—toward spiritual experience.

Our consciousness, therefore, has a different evolutionary direction to the matter of its bodies—the vehicles through which it operates. Like a salmon spawning it has to swim upstream, against the flow, so to speak, and it's this fact that accounts for some of life's friction.

In the early stages of human evolution, the matter and forms around us easily overwhelm our inexperienced consciousness. Swimming against the flow takes considerable determination, and our progress is slow. Without understanding who we really are, we have no reason to defy these "downstream" material desires. In the middle stages of human evolution, as our consciousness develops and our will strengthens, the friction between desire and will starts to get serious. This is where we slowly realize that it's our desires that cause our suffering, and we apply our will to subdue them. This, then, is the core issue of human evolution, this long tug of war between desire and will. It's another good reason to "know thyself," because if your Volvo's going one way, and you're supposed to be going the other, you're in trouble. Will, fortunately, is stronger than desire—which shows how strong will can be—and given enough time, and enough battles, it's will that triumphs. In the latter stages of human evolution, we transcend our "downstream" desires, and our higher self holds the steering wheel uncontested.

Whatever stage you're at now, however the weight of desire, ignorance, and fear holds you back, evolution guarantees that you'll rise to ever greater heights. The Laws of Nature give you the ability to choose who you wish to be and what your world will be. Add to this self-control and the self-direction of a strong moral compass, and you can really begin to enjoy your evolution—undoubtedly the most fascinating, dramatic, and purposeful show on Earth.

Extroduction

So if someone asks "Who are you?" you can choose from any of the following suggestions, or add one of your own: Son of God, Daughter of God, Seed of the Enfolded All, or Apprentice Deity perhaps? But don't let it swell your head, because every other entity in the cosmos is, too.

Enfolded within you, waiting to unfold, is all the beauty, capacity, wisdom, and power of the cosmos. What's more, you're on a Ferris wheel designed to do precisely that. Stretching out before you is an evolutionary path of unimaginable opportunity, wonder, and fun. You have will, so you can choose your thoughts, feelings, and actions. You have the power to create inevitability—the karma of your choice through the power of your will. You have an infinite capacity to do, be, associate with, and experience whatever you will. You're so empowered, it's scary.

And so ends our tour. I hope it's been fun, and I hope it contributes to the value of your afterlife. You're free to zoom! But before you go, remember that this tour and commentary is—like everything else—evolving. This is only what we know today. Tomorrow, we'll undoubtedly know much more, and the day after that we'll have some rewriting to do. But even if we have to rewrite major portions, the revisions can only be better!

Acknowledgments

I wish to express my respect and
gratitude to all the great commu-
nicators of the ancient wisdom,
with special thanks to Charles W.
Leadbeater, Omraam Mikhael
Aivanhov, Annie Besant, and
Bhagavan Das.

Thank you to my wonderful
wife, Deborah Kytic, and my great
friend, Tony Bakusic, without
whose support, love, and encour-
agement this project may never

have materialized. Thank you to my Mum and Dad, who instilled in me a love of nature and gave me the freedom to think for myself.

I also wish to state that drawing a parallel between a Volvo and that wonderful vehicle of consciousness known as the physical body is an enormous compliment.

And now for the real names

Throughout the book the chakras were given names loosely corresponding to their physical position. This was done for simplicity.

As those were only nicknames, here are their real (Sanskrit) names:

Crown chakra	Sahasrara
Brow chakra	Ajna
Throat chakra	Vishuddi
Heart chakra	Anahata
Solar Plexus chakra	Manipura

Sacral chakra	Svadisthana
Base chakra	Muladhara

Recommended reading

Powell, A. E. *The Astral Body.*
Wheaton, IL: Quest Books,
1927. A valuable resource on the
astral plane, compiled and condensed from the works of a number of Theosophical authors.

Krishnamurti, J. *At the Feet of the
Master.* Adyar, Madras, India:
Theosophical Publishing
House, 1910. A beautifully
written and concise treatise
on walking the spiritual path.

Gribbin, John. *Almost Everyone's Guide to Science.* London: Weidenfeld and Nicholson, 1998. If you want to explore nature you need a solid foundation. Fascinating and accessible.

Algeo, John. *Reincarnation Explained.* Wheaton, IL: Quest Books, 1987. A thoughtful and reasoned exploration of reincarnation from a modern point of view.

Aivanhov, Omraam Mikhael. *Cosmic Moral Law.* Frejus, France: 1999. A great spiritual master with an elegant and simple style.

Besant, Annie. *The Ancient Wisdom.* Adyar, Madras, India: Theosophical Publishing House, 1897. A classic of Theosophical wisdom from a remarkable woman.

Besant, A., and C. W. Leadbeater. *Thought Forms.* Adyar, Madras, India: Theosophical Publishing House, 1901. Clairvoyant observation of thoughtforms by two exceptional spiritual teachers. Illustrated.

Frenette, Louise-Marie. *Omraam Mikhael Aivanhov— A Biography.* Liverpool, UK: Suryoma, 1999. A well-researched and absorbing biography of a great spiritual master.

Index

☽ Order Llewellyn Books Today!

Llewellyn publishes hundreds of books on your favorite subjects!
To get these exciting books, including the ones on the following pages,
check your local bookstore or order them directly from Llewellyn.

Order Online

Visit our website at www.llewellyn.com, select your books, and order them on our secure server.

Order By Phone

· Call toll-free within the U.S. at 1-877-NEW-WRLD (1-877-639-9753). Call toll-free within Canada at 1-866-NEW-WRLD (1-866-639-9753)
· We accept VISA, MasterCard, and American Express

Order By Mail

Send the full price of your order (MN residents add 7% sales tax) in U.S. funds, plus postage & handling to:

Llewellyn Worldwide
P.O. Box 64383, Dept. 0-7387-0426-1
St. Paul, MN 55164-0383, U.S.A.

Postage & Handling

Standard (U.S., Mexico, & Canada)
If your order is: Up to $25.00, add $3.50. $25.01–$48.99, add $4.00. $49.00 and over, free standard shipping. (Continental U.S. orders ship UPS. AK, HI, PR, & P.O. Boxes ship USPS 1st class. Mex. and Can. ship PMB.)

International Orders
Surface Mail: For orders of $20.00 or less, add $5 plus $1 per item ordered. For orders of $20.01 and over, add $6 plus $1 per item ordered.

Air Mail: books: Postage and handling is equal to the total retail price of all books in the order. non-book items: Add $5 for each item.

Orders are processed within 2 business days.
Please allow for normal shipping time.
Postage and handling rates subject to change.

Journey of Souls
Case Studies of Life Between Lives

Michael Newton, Ph.D.

This remarkable book uncovers—for the first time—the mystery of life in the spirit world after death on earth. Dr. Michael Newton, a hypnotherapist in private practice, has developed his own hypnosis technique to reach his subjects' hidden memories of the hereafter. The narrative is woven as a progressive travel log around the accounts of twenty-nine people who were placed in a state of superconsciousness. While in deep hypnosis, these subjects describe what has happened to them between their former reincarnations on earth. They reveal graphic details about how it feels to die, who meets us right after death, what the spirit world is really like, where we go and what we do as souls, and why we choose to come back in certain bodies.

After reading *Journey of Souls*, you will acquire a better understanding of the immortality of the human soul. Plus, you will meet day-to-day personal challenges with a greater sense of purpose as you begin to understand the reasons behind events in your own life.

1-56718-485-5
288 pp., 6 x 9 $14.95

Destiny of Souls
New Case Studies of Life Between Lives

Michael Newton, Ph.D.

A pioneer in uncovering the secrets of life, internationally recognized spiritual hypnotherapist Dr. Michael Newton takes you once again into the heart of the spirit world. His groundbreaking research was first published in the best-selling *Journey of Souls*, the definitive study on the afterlife. Now, in *Destiny of Souls*, the saga continues with seventy case histories of real people who were regressed into their lives between lives. Dr. Newton answers the requests of the thousands of readers of the first book who wanted more details about various aspects of life on the other side.

  Destiny of Souls is also designed for the enjoyment of first-time readers who haven't read *Journey of Souls*.

1-56718-499-5
384 pp., 6 x 9, illus. $14.95

also available in Spanish!

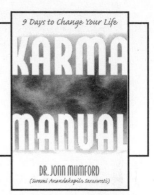

9 Days to Change Your Life

KARMA MANUAL

DR. JONN MUMFORD
(swami Anandakapila Saraswati)

The Karma Manual
9 Days to Change Your Life

Dr. Jonn Mumford (Swami Anandakapila Saraswati)

Many Westerners talk about karma, but few really know much about it. Now Dr. Jonn Mumford provides a clear, practical guide, featuring the traditional yet innovative approach of his first guru, Dr. Swami Gitananda Giti of India.

Karma is a simple law of consequence, not of moralistic retribution and penalty. It's a way of viewing existence that results in increased mental health and self-responsibility.

Discover the different types of karma. Process your personal karma by clearing out unwanted automatic actions—thus lessening the amount and rate at which new karma accumulates. Finally, learn a very direct method for "deep frying" the karmic seeds in your being through the Nine-Day Karma Clearing Program.

1-56718-490-1
216 pp., 5³⁄₁₆ x 8   **$9.95**

A Chakra & Kundalini Workbook

Psycho-Spiritual Techniques for Health, Rejuvenation, Psychic Powers and Spiritual Realization

Dr. Jonn Mumford

Spend just a few minutes each day on the remarkable psycho-physiological techniques in this book and you will quickly build a solid experience of drugless inner relaxation that will lead toward better health, a longer life, and greater control over your personal destiny. Furthermore, you will lay a firm foundation for the subsequent chapters leading to the attainment of supernormal powers (i.e., photographic memory, self-anesthesia, and mental calculations), an enriched inner life, and ultimate transcendence.

A Chakra & Kundalini Workbook is one of the clearest, most approachable books on yoga there is. Tailored for the Western mind, this is a practical system of personal training suited for anyone in today's active and complex world.

1-56718-473-1
296 pp., 7 x 10, 8 color plates   **$17.95**

Kundalini and the Chakras
A Practical Manual—
Evolution in this Lifetime
Genevieve Paulson

The mysteries of Kundalini revealed! We all possess the powerful evolutionary force of Kundalini that can open us to genius states, psychic powers, and cosmic consciousness. As the energies of the Aquarian Age intensify, more and more people are experiencing the "big release" spontaneously but have been ill-equipped to channel its force in a productive manner. This book shows you how to release Kundalini gradually and safely, and is your guide to sating the strange, new appetites which result when life-in-process "blows open" your body's many energy centers.

The section on chakras brings new understanding to these "dials" on our life machine (body). It is the most comprehensive information available for cleansing and developing the chakras and their energies. Read *Kundalini and the Chakras* and prepare to make a quantum leap in your spiritual growth!

0-87542-592-5
224 pp., 6 x 9, illus., color plates $14.95

Chakras for Beginners
A Guide to Balancing Your Chakra Energies

David Pond

The chakras are spinning vortexes of energy located just in front of your spine and positioned from the tailbone to the crown of the head. The freedom with which energy can flow back and forth between you and the universe correlates directly to your total health and well-being.

Blocks or restrictions in this energy flow are expressed as disease, discomfort, lack of energy, fear, or as emotional imbalance. By acquainting yourself with the chakra system, how they work and how they should operate optimally, you can perceive your own blocks and restrictions and develop guidelines for relieving entanglements. The chakras stand out as the most useful model for you to identify how your energy is expressing itself. With *Chakras for Beginners* you will discover what is causing any imbalances, how to bring your energies back into alignment, and how to achieve higher levels of consciousness.

1-56718-537-1
216 pp., 5³⁄₁₆ x 8 $9.95

To order, call 1-877-NEW-WRLD
Prices subject to change without notice

To Write to the Author

If you wish to contact the author or would like more information about this book, please write to the author in care of Llewellyn Worldwide and we will forward your request. Both the author and publisher appreciate hearing from you and learning of your enjoyment of this book and how it has helped you. Llewellyn Worldwide cannot guarantee that every letter written to the author can be answered, but all will be forwarded. Please write to:

David Staume
℅ Llewellyn Worldwide
P.O. Box 64383, Dept. 0-7387-0426-1
St. Paul, MN 55164-0383, U.S.A.

Please enclose a self-addressed stamped envelope for reply, or $1.00 to cover costs. If outside U.S.A., enclose international postal reply coupon.

Many of Llewellyn's authors have websites with additional information and resources. For more information, please visit our website:

http://www.llewellyn.com